The Expert Witness Marketing Book

The Expert Witness Marketing Book

How to Promote
Your Forensic Practice
In a Professional and
Cost-Effective Manner

ROSALIE HAMILTON

EXPERT COMMUNICATIONS
Expert Witness Marketing & Training

Published by:
Expert Communications
140 Island Way, #288
Clearwater, FL 33767
Telephone: 727-467-0700; Toll Free: 866-467-0801
Fax: 727-467-0800
Web site: http://www.expertcommunications.com
e-mail: rhamilton@expertcommunications.com

Typeset, printed, and bound
in the United States of America

First Edition 2003

**Library of Congress
Cataloging-in-Publication Data**

Hamilton, Rosalie, (Rosalie R.)
     The expert witness marketing book : how to promote
your forensic practice in a professional and cost-effective
manner / by Rosalie Hamilton. – 1st ed.
     p.cm.
     Includes index.
     LCCN 2002094889
     ISBN 0-9723237-3-2

     1. Evidence, Expert–United States–Marketing.
     2. Forensic sciences–United States. I. Title.

     KF8961.Z9H362003
     347.73'067'0688   QBI02-200724

*Cover design and interior design
and composition by Cynthia Pinsonnault,
Graphic Bytes – www.graphicbytes.net.*

DISCLAIMERS

This book outlines a plan for marketing a forensic practice and how to implement the plan. It would be impossible to communicate in one book all there is to know about legal marketing, much less all of the principles of marketing, so omissions are likely. Generally accepted marketing principles are reliable in most situations, but there will always be exceptions.

An attempt has been made to provide a great deal of resource information for the expert witness in the Appendix. The inclusion of certain references and the exclusion of others reflect only the impossibility of listing all those that exist.

This book is not intended to give legal advice. An expert witness may require the services of an attorney for his practice.

The author, Rosalie Hamilton, and the publisher, Expert Communications, shall have neither liability nor responsibility to any person or entity with respect to any loss or damage caused or alleged to be caused directly or indirectly by the information contained in this book.

In this communication age, information changes constantly. The author apologizes for the unintentional inclusion of any obsolete information.

Personal Disclaimer to Women from the Author

I have worked with experts on a daily basis for several years. Many are women, several of whom have become my personal friends. I am pleased to report that the population of law schools and many other professional schools today is almost 50% female.

For simplicity, I have used "he," "him," and "his" throughout the book. Women readers, please overlook this usage. I look forward to a day when words will be coined in our society that apply to either gender. As a professional who entered the workforce when certain jobs were denied me because of gender and who has achieved some degree of success, I let the present lack of appropriate pronouns bother me "all the way to the bank." Please do likewise. I hope the book aids you in becoming even more successful than you already are.

TABLE OF CONTENTS

ACKNOWLEDGEMENTS

When a busy person decides to write a book, friends, family, and associates must pitch in for the book to become a reality.

My greatest debt of gratitude is to Dan Poynter, parachute expert and publishing guru, and Dr. David Benjamin, expert in toxicology and the art of expert witnessing, for sharing knowledge and inspiration.

Cynthia Pinsonnault of Graphic Bytes in Houston magically turned the manuscript into a book to be printed and also designed and produced the cover. Meredith Hamilton, editor extraordinaire and my daughter and friend, edited the book, along with Sally Koch, Vice President of SmartNetworker, Inc., who worked it into her spare time between midnight and morning. Sandra Simmons did the proofreading.

Steve Babitsky of SEAK, Inc. encouraged me to write the book, as did Betty Lipscher of the National Forensic Center, the housemother of the expert witness fraternity. Jim Robinson, Esq., President of www.jurispro.com, the Internet expert witness directory, was supportive and helpful as an attorney, a member of the expert witness professional community, and as a friend. Dr. Dean Noble, founder of one of the first Internet expert witness directories, now www.experts.com, was generous in contributing information about the Internet.

Anne Galvi, M.D., working with Charles Gauntt, M.D., Orthopedic Surgeon, was particularly helpful in reviewing and in sharing a doctor's viewpoint. Wilma Couch, R.N., Directory of Med-Expertise, L.L.C., medical referral service, added gems of wisdom mined from experience.

I received invaluable help from peer reviewers Paul Adkins, Managing Partner, West Coast Accident Recon Practice; Dan Jackson, CPA, CMC, CFE, Principal, AlixPartners; Jim Misselwitz, Vice President of ECBM Insurance; Melissa Nelson, Director of Marketing for Nelson Architectural Engineers; Garth Budlong, Advertising Consultant at *Texas Lawyer;* John and Alice Oakley, the marketing professionals behind Robert Hughes Associates, Inc., insurance consultants; Ron Penner, Web designer par excellence at CityCent.com; Rodney Richmond, pharmacy expert; Ron Russ, computer expert; and Jerry Williams, P.E., engineering and construction expert.

Last, but not least, thanks to friends Kay Proctor of talktogov.com, JoSandra Greenberg, the consummate English teacher, and Doris Booth, of Authorlink, for personal inspiration, as well as my sister Linda Johnston, my son Barry Hamilton, and his wife Lisa, sometimes my assistants and, delightfully, also my friends.

I wish to pay special tribute to Dennis Weber, Advertising Consultant at *Texas Lawyer*. Dennis was one of the first people to recognize the scope of expert witness marketing.

OPENING STATEMENTS

CHAPTER ONE GUIDE

- What is marketing?
- What does the book cover?
- How do I use the book?
- How do I get started?

∽ Providing litigation support and possibly deposition and court testimony can be a challenging and satisfying extension to a successful career. It can also become a profitable business and should be planned, marketed, and managed like a business. Along with your integrity and the quality of service you offer, marketing is the key element in developing a profitable business.

You may, however, have begun your career life in a profession in which marketing, much less advertising, was considered a taboo subject. Perhaps, by virtue of working as an employee in business, science, or academia, you have never needed to create a business plan or marketing strategy.

∼ *The Expert Witness Marketing Book* will give you the knowledge and skills to effectively communicate to the legal community the value and availability of your professional services.

You have dedicated your life to becoming an expert in your field. You simply need to convey the expertise that your education and experience have created and how your insight and understanding will be of benefit in legal proceedings.

Promoting to the general public, however, is one thing; marketing professional services to another professional and often sophisticated service community is another. Factor in the uniqueness of the legal fraternity, and the rationale for *The Expert Witness Marketing Book* becomes clear.

WHAT IS MARKETING?

The dictionary definition of marketing is the process or technique of promoting, selling, and distributing a product or service. Promoting is communication. Selling, especially in a market in which traditional selling is inappropriate, is communication. Distributing, or delivering the service of litigation support and expert testimony, is communication. It is *all* communication.

The author of the wonderful book, *Selling the Invisible: A Field Guide to Modern Marketing*, Henry Beckwith, who is also an attorney, says, "Communication is not a skill. It is *the* skill."

Whether letting the legal community know that you are able, willing, and ready to help in the litigation process, or speaking in a courtroom, it is all about communication.

Communication occurs in many forms, not just visual and oral. It is accomplished through materials that express who you are and what you have done in your life to qualify as an expert, by how you dress, and by how you speak to people and conduct yourself. Communication is how you convey your integrity and your professionalism.

> ∿ You do not choose to communicate; you are communicating continuously. Communication occurs whether or not you are aware of your message. You can, however, choose to take responsibility for your communication and make it work for you. *The Expert Witness Marketing Book* gives you the tools to do that.

WHAT DOES THE BOOK COVER?

The Expert Witness Marketing Book starts with developing a basic business plan. The earning potential for a litigation support practice is excellent. Treat it as a business and plan it accordingly.

Along with a business plan you need a marketing plan. The word *plan* is emphasized. It is too easy to go off unprepared, printing stationery on your PC that you think looks nice, and buying a little advertising which may or may not be effective and could be detrimental, and then wondering a few months later why the legal community is not beating a path to your door.

After addressing a business plan and a marketing plan, the book goes on to discuss fee setting and composing a contract and other materials you will need. "Why a contract?" you ask. Read the chapter.

The value of creating a database of prospects, clients, and referral sources is explained, along with instructions on how to build it and utilize the data.

Chapter 6, "Basic Business Communications," gives tips on choosing materials that communicate for you in a positive way, along with budget suggestions. This chapter comments on tailoring your *curriculum vitae* for the legal market. It also addresses the expert's appearance and the part it plays in communicating.

If there is a key chapter in *The Expert Witness Marketing Book*, it is "Networking – *The Key to Your Success*." Referral is the primary method by which attorneys locate expert witnesses. You must master the art of networking: the developing of contacts or exchanging of information with others in an informal network.

Publicity, whether writing, speaking, or communicating newsworthy items about yourself or your services, is a primary promotional strategy. A number of methods are introduced and explained.

The chapter on direct mail explains the differences in types of mailings, provides postal information, and discusses sending newsletters.

The good, the bad, and the ugly are presented in "Referral Services – *How They Work*." This chapter defines the scope of referral services, how they work, and typical financial arrangements.

The chapter on advertising describes types of advertising and spending guidelines.

Directory listing is one of the most effective advertising venues for expert witnesses. A complete chapter is devoted to what the expert should know about print directories.

The Internet chapter is extensive, encompassing many areas, from reserving a site domain name and developing a personal Web site, to choosing the best Internet expert witness directories in which to list.

For most expert witnesses the insurance industry is a potential source of business in addition to the legal field. The chapter on insurance details how to find the decision makers, and addresses advertising and networking in this market.

HOW DO I USE THE BOOK?

Read *The Expert Witness Marketing Book* straight through the first time. Many of the marketing steps overlap, and you will see how they relate to one another.

For instance, your image and appearance, which are discussed in "Basic Business Communications," are critical subjects for your consideration in networking, covered in a separate chapter. Professional announcements and news releases, included in "Publicity," are items that can be printed in legal publications and also sent out as promotional mailings, explained in the chapter on direct mail. The information in "Referral Services" is pertinent to the recommendations in the insurance chapter, particularly regarding services that secure contracts for physicians to do independent medical evaluations. Expert witness directories are published in print, which is covered in the chapter on directory listings, and on the Internet, which is described in the Internet marketing chapter.

After going through the text once, begin again, assembling your marketing plan, step by step. An outline is provided at the beginning of each chapter for your use as a guide. The book is meant to be a workbook. Mark the pages and cross-reference chapters to other chapters.

You do not have to master every marketing skill at once. Revisit chapters and parts of chapters to evaluate your progress.

HOW DO I GET STARTED?

The book is designed not only to give you the strategy and tactics of communicating your litigation support services, but also to convince you that you can do it and motivate you to take action.

You have invested a lifetime of time and energy in your occupational field, not in marketing. Marketing is an expertise of its own, *which you can learn*. Read the book, write a plan, and set a budget. You are not expected to act on every suggestion, especially in the beginning. Implement basic steps as they apply to your particular situation, and then add other projects and activities as they seem appropriate.

As your litigation support business grows and you begin to master not only the marketing of your practice but also the business of law, read the book again. You will discover that you have acquired a clearer understanding of how various marketing activities fit together and contribute to your success. You might even be surprised to discover that you enjoy practicing your newly found skills in communication and creativity.

PLANNING

Your Road Map to Success

CHAPTER TWO GUIDE

- Business Plan
  - Legal Issues
  - Business Name
  - Location
  - Financial Needs
  - Services
  - Clients
  - Competition
  - Fees
  - Service Delivery
- Composing Your Business Plan
- The Why in Your Business Plan
- Marketing Plan
  - Image
  - Communication
- Creating Your Marketing Plan
- Marketing as Public Relations

To establish your business you need a business plan and a marketing plan. A business plan is simply a description of your business and how you will operate it. A marketing plan is your communication strategy. Although our focus is on creating an initial program of action, bear in mind that your marketing plan, as well as certain elements of your business plan, may change over time. The cycle is evaluate-plan-execute-evaluate. Therefore, even if your practice is a one-person operation, write your plans. Having your thoughts on paper will make evaluating and adjusting your plans later easier and more meaningful.

BUSINESS PLAN

Business plans are developed primarily for two reasons – 1) to provide data to funding sources and 2) to plot a course of action. Most likely, your litigation support business will not require outside financing. Your objective in composing a business plan, therefore, is to create a road map, to make certain you are going where you want to go and to avoid potholes in the road.

Most of the information in books on writing business plans focuses on convincing funding sources of the viability of your business. Nonetheless, you can pick up valuable pointers from reading such books as *Business Plans for Dummies*, by Paul Tiffany, PH.D., and Steven D. Peterson, PH.D.

Along with addressing strictly business issues, consider the impact of a start-up business on the increase in your work hours, possible strain on family relationships, and even irritability due to working two jobs for a while. These considerations do not mean that a person should despair of trying to expand into an additional practice (forensic). They simply underscore the fact that a start-up business is that – a business – with the attendant need for planning.

Legal Issues

- Which legal form is best for you – a sole proprietorship, a partnership, or a corporation? This is a subject best discussed with your attorney, which begs the following question:
- Do you need a business attorney? I recommend at a minimum that you engage an attorney to write or review your contract and other engagement materials.
- Will you need professional liability insurance such as errors and omissions? This is also a subject to discuss with your attorney. It is addressed in the chapter on composing your contract.

Business Name

Will you create a business name, or will you market your services under your personal name? Unless you have employees or a substantial group of contractors, or expect to in the future, you do not need a firm name. You can work under just your name, or your business name can be John J. Anderson, [whatever legal form designation, e.g., LLC]. Alternately, you can use your own name and also indicate the type of business, such as John Anderson Robotics Consulting. Using your personal name by itself or as a business name, such as John Anderson & Associates, could be a limiting factor if you try to sell your practice.

Choosing a business name that indicates the type of service in consulting work is helpful, but also has a potential downside. If you later modify your service offerings or vastly expand them, the name may no longer be appropriate. Choose a name that will work as you grow. You can describe the service in a tagline after your name.

Legal work is not the forum for cute names. Also, ensure (unless the name is yours and just happens to be difficult) that the name is pronounceable and simple to spell.

Some people feel so strongly about coming up near the top in alphabetical listings that they end up in a list of AAA's, ABC's,

Acme's, and Advanced's that is so daunting a reader might skip that section entirely!

Beware of using a geographic name, such as Northeast Environmental. A geographic name might be appropriate when you establish the business, but can be limiting if you later choose to expand into other markets.

Your business name should convey the image you wish to reflect. *Branding* is the message communicated to your public by your business name, the tagline that describes your business, and possibly a logo, or mark. That brand is what comes to mind when people think of you and your services. Choose a name carefully.

Do not forget the legal requirements, such as registering your business name at the office of your Secretary of State. Better safe than sorry (voice of experience): Check the availability of your chosen name before using it and having it printed on costly materials. Also determine whether the name or a related version is available as an Internet domain name. This can be critical.

Location

Will you work at your residence, acquire an outside office, or build your forensic practice from a current employment location? Addressing this question involves business, personal, and economic considerations too numerous to list here. Consult with your attorney, your accountant, your employer, prospective employees and contractors, and your family.

Financial Needs

Where will you acquire the funds for start-up costs? How much money will you need? At the beginning of your consulting practice there will be up-front costs for business cards, stationery, and perhaps brochures. You may want to develop a Web site right away so that the domain address can be listed on all of your materials. If you do not have an up-to-date computer system, you should acquire one. You may want prospect and client management software. Marketing costs, which will be ongoing, will include expert witness directory listings and advertising, conferences and workshops, and possibly attorney mailing lists and mailing services.

One decision at this stage of your plan is whether you want your expert witness/consulting practice to become a substantial part of your employment. You may want to develop litigation consulting into a second career when you retire. That decision will determine how large an investment you should dedicate to the start-up of your consulting business.

If you are going into litigation support full-time (not recommended unless you are retired), are your living expenses provided from another source for several months or even a year?

Services

What services will you offer or exclude? In addition to the parameters of an expert's capabilities, his decision of what services to deliver to attorneys may involve excluding certain tasks for which he is qualified.

For example, a physician, early or late in his consulting career, might determine that he does not enjoy deposition or court testimony and therefore only wants to review medical records. If so, he needs to specify that point in advertising or directory listings, or perhaps work on litigation matters only through medical referral agencies. In addition, a physician may or may not want to conduct independent medical evaluations (IMEs).

Even if your regular service includes the possibility of testimony, if you are approached on a case on which your identification would create conflict for you, e.g., community disapproval, you can limit your work to that of a consultant, whose work is not discoverable because he renders only verbal opinions.

After a physician retires from active practice, most law firms will not hire him to review cases because the court might not admit his testimony. His options then are to contract with law firms or insurance companies to do medical record review only.

Engineers might conduct accident investigations, but not perform reconstruction. An engineer could possibly have a laboratory or testing facilities, or at least access to them, or out-source that part of his service.

In addition to consulting in their own specialties, experts can offer the service of locating experts in other fields for the attorney.

Often an expert wants to help the attorney develop the case, not just consult on a particular issue. Actually, in many, perhaps a majority of cases, attorneys should consult with the expert from the beginning and use him later in such areas as developing the cross-examination of the opposing expert regarding the technical issues involved. Unfortunately, budget considerations generally rule, as does arrogance occasionally on the part of the attorney, and the expert's assistance is not utilized. Offer anyway, so the attorney knows help is available.

Clients

Who will be interested in your services? If you are an expert witness/consultant, the obvious answer is attorneys. The next question is whether you will offer your services to both plaintiff and defense attorneys. In deposition and in court you will appear to be more objective if you have served both sides. In actual practice, your record may become skewed to one side. As a professional member of a field you may feel uncomfortable testifying against another member of your group. If you have spent the majority of your career working for a government entity, the defense may be reluctant to call you, or you may actually feel biased and not want to work on the defense side.

One expert criminologist has testified for so many defendants that prosecutors refuse to use him, regardless of his objectivity.

Because you will almost certainly be asked by the opposing attorney whether you have worked on both plaintiff and defense cases, I recommend, even if you work mostly on one side or even prefer one side, that you try to work for the other side on at least a few cases. Although you should not, of course, take a case that you cannot support, encourage referrals by letting your associates know that you are open to working on the other side. When a case becomes available from your untypical side that you can in good conscience support, actively pursue the engagement.

Which groups you choose as your prospective markets will influence your advertising decisions. If you are trying to reach defense attorneys, for instance, placing an advertisement or classified listing in your state's defense attorney association magazine may be more effective for you than placing it in the state bar association magazine.

Part of your marketing plan should be a determination of whether there are other businesses, such as insurance companies, that can use your services. Comments and suggestions regarding working for insurance companies and adjusters are included in the chapter, "Insurance Companies – *Another Potential Source of Business.*"

Competition

Who is your competition, and how do you compare? Considering that most cases requiring an expert witness involve at least two experts and our society shows no signs of becoming less litigious, competition should not be your primary concern in building an expert practice. You will learn valuable lessons, however, from analyzing the practices of two or three experts in your field. Study their professional qualifications, appearance, communication skills, and reputation among their peers, and note how they market themselves and the fees they charge.

EXPERT WITNESS MARKETING
WHAT, WHO, AND WHY

By Rosalie Hamilton of Expert Communications

When a professional decides to market his services as an expert witness, he sometimes places too much emphasis on the "what" and too little on the "who" and "why."

The "what you are" is the information you list in directories and other advertising. It includes your area of specialty, education, experience, and other credentials. This data communicates to attorneys that you are qualified, and that you are available for litigation work. It comprises your qualifications for forensic work, but likely there are several, perhaps many, experts in your specialty with your degree(s) or better, and experience of similar value.

The "who you are" is what you must also make known to the legal community. You can publicize your expertise in many ways and, by so doing, communicate your personality, working style and the like, through teaching, writing, and speaking, to name just a few. The most important opportunities are networking functions that allow you to meet and talk with attorneys or with other people who can refer you to attorneys. This is where your communication skills really come into play, as they reflect what you will be like to work with and how you will be perceived in deposition and in court.

Analysis of the "why an attorney should hire *you*" is one of the most important components of your marketing plan, yet it is rarely made. It is integral that you know why you are the best choice. What do you know about yourself, that were the attorney to know, he would certainly pick you? Rarely does that reason relate to your credentials. It is to be found, instead, in a candid and comprehensive analysis of your personal strengths and weaknesses, especially in regard to your competitors.

Are you thorough in your work? Are you punctual for appointments and in meeting deadlines? Are you easy to work with, flexible? Do you listen effectively?

Henry Beckwith, in his book, *Selling the Invisible: A Field Guide to Modern Marketing,* says, "In most professional services, you are not really selling your expertise, because your expertise is assumed, and because your prospective client cannot intelligently evaluate your expertise anyway. Instead, you are selling a *relationship*. And in most cases, that is where you need the most work. If you're selling a service, you're selling a relationship."

After synthesizing the qualities that compose your uniqueness, look honestly at whether you are working to improve on or overcome your weaknesses. Also, do you know how to capitalize on and communicate your strengths?

When the attorney has compiled a list of experts and calls each of them for a *c.v.*, or when he calls to determine your suitability for and interest in working on a case, the impression you make on him will weigh more than will a slight difference in credentials between you and your competition.

The "why [you]," therefore, should be determined as you begin creating your marketing plan. You will not only express the "why" in the "who" of your program and sometimes even in the "what," but, more importantly, the "why" may be the variable that leads to successful engagements.

***

After objectively assessing your own strengths and weaknesses, determine your competitive advantage. Is your education or professional experience superior? If you are not a novice, have you handled a greater number of cases, or bigger or more successful cases, or have you worked with prestigious law firms? Do you present yourself more professionally or appear more credible? Are there exclusive dimensions to your expertise? What comprises your personal uniqueness and, therefore, your competitive edge?

A competitive advantage can be only a perceived advantage. You can use this to your benefit. A large engineering firm may have many different specialties of engineers, along with its own testing facilities. Alternately, a sole practitioner engineer can promote himself as being more responsive to the attorney, more personally involved in each case, and possibly less costly. Learn to articulate your competitive advantage in a professional manner.

Fees

What prices will you charge? A separate chapter, "Fees – *I Enjoy My Work, but I Don't Work for the Fun of It*," is devoted to this discussion.

Also, note *The Guide to Experts' Fees*, a book listed in the Resources section. The National Forensic Center sent questionnaires to randomly selected experts listed in the *Forensic Services Directory* to ascertain their current charges and fees. The result is this valuable survey of experts' fees in many different fields.

Service Delivery

How will you deliver your services? To help you answer this essential question I refer you to the "how-to" books on working as an expert witness, which are listed in the Resources section. Three of the most popular ones are *Succeeding as an Expert Witness*, *The Expert Witness Handbook*, and *The Comprehensive Forensic Services Manual*.

They cover such topics as the expert's relationship with the attorney, the investigative process, the expert's role in the discovery process, report writing, legal procedures, the challenges of testifying, and ethical standards for an expert witness.

COMPOSING YOUR BUSINESS PLAN

Plans are like goals – if they are not written, they are wishes. Compose a list of what has to be done, beginning with the above steps. Write down the start-up tasks that have to be accomplished, how they are to be done, and the time frame in which to accomplish them.

Assess the resources available to you, such as family members pitching in to help. Do not hesitate to ask; people are usually more willing to help than you expect.

Be realistic about your limitations. If you are already working 50 hours per week, something has to be sacrificed for you to temporarily increase your workload. It may be your regular work, or your family or recreational time, or, often, it is an executive's or other professional's sleeping time. Whatever you determine, realize the necessity of making a time commitment.

THE WHY IN YOUR BUSINESS PLAN

As in goal setting, the essential point in developing a business plan is often neglected – the reason you are doing this. If you articulate clearly for yourself why you want to build a forensic practice, then when you get bogged down trying to organize your business or the engagements seem slow in coming in, you will be less likely to become discouraged.

How will you benefit *personally* from becoming an expert witness? Consider what you want to gain from building or increasing your litigation support business – full-time or part-time work, supplemental or maximum income, retirement activity and/or income, intellectual stimulation, or something else.

A number of my marketing clients, when they decide to pursue or expand a forensic career, are in a time of reflection as to where they are in life and what they want to do with the remainder. Becoming a legal expert can be a fitting capstone to a lifetime of achievements in a particular discipline and may provide its own justification.

MARKETING PLAN

Marketing *is* a plan. Marketing comprises the majority of your business plan, and the key to effective marketing is strategy. Advertising is the creative part, but marketing is literally a plan – how to communicate the availability and the value of your services.

Image

What image do you want to create of yourself and your business? A subject unto itself – see notes on image and appearance in the chapter on basic business communications.

Communication

How will you let prospective clients know that you are available and qualified? The major avenues for promoting yourself to attorneys are:

- Word-of-Mouth (Networking)
- Publicity
- Professional Announcements
- Direct Mail
- Your Own Web site
- Internet Expert Witness Directories
- Print Expert Witness Directories
- Classified Advertising
- Display Advertising
- Expert Witness Referral Services
- Newsletters

CREATING YOUR MARKETING PLAN

After reading through the book, list the communication steps you want to take first, just as for your business plan. Make a notation for each marketing avenue. Write a to-do list, with a time frame. For someone new to marketing that time might be the next 90–120 days.

The primary thing is to *do something:* reserve an appropriate domain name, design your business materials, compose an announcement that you have opened a forensic practice, start writing an article of interest to attorneys, register with TASA (Technical Advisory Service for Attorneys), start compiling a database from the business cards you have collected. Do not launch into a possibly overwhelming project in the beginning, such as publishing a newsletter.

After your initial efforts, re-read the book. You will then be ready to incorporate additional activities. You will also better understand the reason behind certain suggestions.

MARKETING AS PUBLIC RELATIONS

All of your marketing, not just publicity activities, creates your public relations position. Public Relations is the creation, shaping, and nurturing of your image in the minds of your public. Marketing is the communication of that image.

First, define your public. *Your* public is not *the* public; it is the segment to whom you want to direct your efforts, in this case, attorneys and their staffs. In a lesser category are your contacts in *the* public who might refer an attorney to you. The majority of your efforts should be aimed at creating positive opinions about you and your services in the legal community.

Public relations activities such as news releases of meritorious awards and actions, accomplishments, and events comprise the news often issued by a public relations professional or a press agent. You probably recognize the value of developing skill in public relations activities. What you might overlook is the impact, both positively and negatively, that other factors have on one's image – factors such as stationery and business cards, physical appearance, manners, communication skills, and even your office.

"Perception is reality" is not just a truism. Nurture and protect a perception that will contribute to your success.

C A U T I O N

If you want to educate yourself further on marketing, choose books that specifically address professional services rather than generic marketing books, which apply mostly to product marketing. Moreover, even within the consulting industry, litigation support is unique. Marketing your services in the field of forensics calls for discretion.

Acquire all of the marketing knowledge you can. Just be forewarned that not all practices should be implemented in the legal field, in which objectivity and the perception of it are the primary benefits you are offering to a prospective client.

FEES

I Enjoy My Work, But I Don't Work for the Fun of It

CHAPTER THREE GUIDE

- Fee Setting
  - Factors in Rate Setting
  - Examples of Fees
- Your Rate
- Billing Charges
  - Fees for Time in Testimony
    - Importance of Advance Payment
  - Deposition Fees
    - Importance of Advance Payment
    - Videotaped Deposition Testimony
  - Expenses
  - Retainer
  - Cancellations and Postponements
- Billing Procedures
- Collections
- Contingency Payment
- Referral Agency Rates
- The Issue of Your Fees During Testimony

ᔫ One of the most frequently asked questions at a meeting of fledgling expert witnesses is, "How do I determine how much to charge for my services?"

FEE SETTING

At the library, at the bookstore, and on the Internet you can find books offering general fee-setting formulas for the person going into business for himself. If a person is leaving a salaried position to become a consultant, the most logical formula is a calculation based on his salary translated into an hourly rate, multiplied by a factor of approximately 3.0. The exponential factor is to cover overhead expenses; benefits customarily paid by an employer, such as insurance premiums and the employer's part of Social Security; and down-time. Kate Kelly points out in her book, *How to Set Your Fees and Get Them*, that a self-employed person should make the factor great enough for time to be spent on administrative matters and marketing, as well as for vacation, holidays, and possibly sick leave.

If you are setting up your own practice after having worked for another person or company, make a detailed list of the services that have been provided to you at no cost. You will now have overhead expenses even if you work out of your house and do most of the administrative tasks yourself. Besides needing a telephone, office equipment, and supplies, you will have postage and delivery expenses, possibly require office help, and will probably pay more taxes and purchase additional insurance. You will need to invest in marketing and advertising as well.

Make certain that the final numbers comprising this formula produce a profit in addition to providing a living. Although the consultant can influence profit by varying his productivity and control of expenses, he may also need to increase the factor.

If a person entering the forensic field is already self-employed in a profession, he can calculate the hourly value of his time when working full-time in his profession and the corresponding loss when he is not on billable time, e.g., in his office or performing surgery.

Ultimately, your rates should be set by the rule of most businesses, which is, *what the market will bear*. There are several considerations that you should take into account in determining your rate for forensic work.

Factors in Rate Setting

Find out what other experts in your forensic field charge. With certain exceptions, you do not want to have the lowest rate or the highest rate. The best position is usually between the middle and the highest.

Obtain rates from several people. Be especially cognizant of geographic differences in rates. One doctor discovered rates for similar IME services as low as $400 on the East Coast and $800–$1500 in the West.

Do your credentials of education, experience, and accomplishment place you in the upper echelon of your profession?

Consider supply and demand – how many people work in your field of expertise?

Are you an effective communicator? Are you skilled in analysis and synthesis? Are you likeable? Will judges and juries deem you trustworthy from your appearance, demeanor, and speech?

Another component of *what the market will bear* is the potential case awards. Plaintiff attorneys working on high-stakes cases expect to pay more than those in low-stakes cases. This is not to suggest that you vary your rates, as you should rarely do so. It is rather that an expert witness who typically testifies in high stakes cases will probably be able to set a high rate.

The expert witness rate for working with a government agency may be regulated. In such instances you may wish to decline the assignment or make an exception to accept a lower rate. Another exception might be a case in which you feel motivated, due to the nature of the case, to work for no fee or a reduced fee. An example is a case involving children or one in which the attorney is also working *pro bono* (free). If the court hires you, it will likely set the expert fees.

Examples of Fees

The Guide to Experts' Fees, published by the National Forensic Center, is listed in the Resources section. This survey, compiled from questionnaires sent to randomly selected experts listed in the *Forensic Services Directory* to ascertain their current charges and fees, will show you a range of rates for various services in many fields.

YOUR RATE

Usually, an expert tends to charge too little rather than too much. Every time that the author has recommended to an expert that he raise his rate, the expert's business has increased. Lawyers perceive from a substantial rate that they are dealing with an important expert. A rate lower than your competition can seem cheaper, not better.

According to marketing guru Dan Kennedy, price is the laziest and riskiest advantage with which to market. Obtaining and keeping business based purely on price is difficult, as it can imply less value or lower quality.

Certainly if you have built a reputation among attorneys as an objective and credible witness who has effective communication skills, you should evaluate your rates periodically. You will probably do so after attending a seminar at which you network with your peers or a CLE class relating to expert witness work. Make a point to review your rates annually, perhaps at year-end along with other administrative tasks, such as tax work. If no prospect ever balks at your rate, it is probably not as high as it could be.

BILLING CHARGES

You can charge an hourly rate, a half-day or full-day rate, or a combination. The half-day rate can be set at four or five hours, or even slightly less than four hours. The full-day rate is generally set equal to an eight or ten-hour day.

Tasks such as telephone conferences are often conducted in small segments, and thus charges can be billed in quarter hours or even tenths of an hour.

Certain services, e.g., independent medical evaluation, can be billed as a flat fee. A tip from Thomas H. Veitch, ESQ., in *The Consultant's Guide to Litigation Services: How to Be an Expert Witness:* "If you do use the flat fee method, be very specific about the precise services that you will render, and have a clear understanding with the client that any work requested beyond the specified services will require additional fee payment."

Whether you charge different rates for record review, phone conferences, office conferences, or report writing is a matter of personal preference. Experts are divided in their opinions as to whether to differentiate or not.

Also a matter of personal choice is whether to charge one rate for preparation work such as investigation or report writing, and a different rate for deposition and court testimony. Forensic firms may charge different rates for work performed by their associates with lesser credentials, such as research, just as attorneys usually charge a reduced rate for their paralegals' work.

For work done outside their offices, most experts charge for their time on a portal-to-portal basis, that is, from the time they leave their office or home until they return from the engagement. Others, on an overnight engagement, "turn off the meter" at the end of the business day and resume again in the morning. These travel fees are sometimes charged by the hour and sometimes by the day. A few people do not charge for travel time at all. This is a decision that should reflect the considerations outlined above, such as your competitors' rates and what income producing activities you are missing by being away. Discuss overnight arrangements with the client well in advance.

See the example of Rodney Richmond's Appendix A, Fee Schedule and Payment Terms, Depositions and Courtroom Testimony/ Appearances.

The Expert Witness Marketing Book

Within his home state Mr. Richmond charges by the hour, but for testimony taken outside the state he offers a *per diem* rate. His viewpoint is that although he will be gone from home he will not be working twenty-four hours per day, so he feels that charging a daily rate is reasonable. For out-of-state testimony he is still adequately compensated, and attorneys appreciate the consideration.

Imitate attorneys in carefully billing for time spent talking on the telephone and in conducting research. Internet research, in particular, can be quite time-consuming and should be scrupulously recorded and billed.

LITIGATION CONSULTING AGREEMENT

This Agreement is made effective as of **mm/dd/yyyy** by and between **John Smith, Esq.** of **123 Main Street, Suite 100, Anytown, USA 12345** and **Rodney G. Richmond, RPh, MS, FASCP** of **The Mackenzie Group, Ltd. (dba PharmacoLegal Associates),** at **Sherwood Lane, Glade Springs Village, Daniels, WV 25801.**

In this Agreement, the party who is contracting to receive services shall be referred to as "Client," and the party who will be providing the services shall be referred to as "Consultant." Consultant has a background in pharmacy/medication utilization and related services and is willing to provide services to Client based on this background. Client desires to have services provided by Consultant. Therefore, the parties agree as follows:

1. DESCRIPTION OF SERVICES
    Beginning on **mm/dd/yyyy** the Consultant will provide the following generally described services (collectively, the "Services"): review of medical files, answering specific medical questions asked by Client, meeting individually with claims adjusters to provide medical advice on cases, participating in case conferences, and providing medical training to staff. This may include but not be limited to research, analysis, testing, inspection,

review of materials, patient interviews, report preparation, expert testimony in depositions and trial proceedings if necessary, reading and correction of deposition transcript, and review and signing of affidavits and similar documents.

2. PERFORMANCE OF SERVICES
    The manner in which the Services are to be performed, and the specific hours to be worked by Consultant shall be determined by Consultant. Client will rely on Consultant to work as many hours as may be reasonably necessary to fulfill Consultant's obligations under this Agreement.

3. FEE SCHEDULE AND PAYMENT TERMS
    Please see *Appendix A* of this Agreement entitled *Fee Schedule and Payment Terms*.

4. NEW PROJECT APPROVAL
    Consultant and Client recognize that Consultant's Services will include working on various projects for Client. Consultant shall obtain the approval of Client prior to the commencement of a new project.

5. TERMINATION
    Either party through written notice to the other party may terminate this Agreement at any time. However, the terms of the Agreement shall remain in effect until all obligations outlined in this Agreement are fulfilled (e.g., documents, equipment or other materials referenced in Paragraph 12 are returned to Client; all outstanding invoices are paid in full to Consultant; etc.).

6. RELATIONSHIP OF PARTIES
    It is understood by the parties that Consultant is an independent contractor with respect to Client, and not an employee of Client. Client will not provide fringe benefits, including health insurance benefits, paid vacation, or any other employee benefit, for the benefit of Consultant.

7. DISCLOSURE
    Consultant is required to disclose any outside activities or interests, including ownership or participation in the development of prior inventions, that conflict or may conflict with the best interests of Client. Prompt disclosure is required under this paragraph if the activity or interest is related, directly or indirectly, to any activity that Consultant may be involved with on behalf of Client.

Client Initials: _____
Consultant Initials: _____

The Expert Witness Marketing Book

8. INJURIES

Consultant acknowledges Consultant's obligation to obtain appropriate insurance coverage for the benefit of Consultant (and Consultant's employees, if any). Consultant waives any rights to recovery from Client for any injuries that Consultant (and/or Consultant's employees) may sustain while performing services under this Agreement and that are a result of the negligence of Consultant or Consultant's employees.

9. INDEMNIFICATION

Client agrees to indemnify and hold Consultant harmless from all claims, losses, expenses, and fees including attorney fees, costs, and judgments that may be asserted against Consultant that result from the acts of omissions of Client, Client's employees, if any, and Client's agents.

10. ASSIGNMENT

Consultant's obligations under this Agreement may not be assigned or transferred to any other person, firm, or corporation without the prior written consent of Client.

11. CONFIDENTIALITY

Client recognizes that Consultant has and will have the following types of information, but not limited to, including: products, future plans, business affairs, process information, trade secrets, technical information, customer lists, product design information, and other proprietary information (collectively "Information") which are valuable, special, and unique assets of Client and need to be protected from improper disclosure. In consideration for the disclosure of the Information, Consultant agrees that Consultant will not at any time or in any manner, either directly or indirectly, use any Information for Consultant's own benefit, or divulge, disclose, or communicate in any manner any Information to any third party without the prior written consent of Client. Consultant will protect the Information and treat it as strictly confidential. A violation of this paragraph shall be a material violation of this Agreement.

12. RETURN OF RECORDS

Upon termination of this Agreement, Consultant shall deliver all records, notes, data, memoranda, models, and equipment of any nature that are in Consultant's possession or under Consultant's control and that are Client's property or relate to Client's business.

Client Initials: _____
Consultant Initials: _____

13. NOTICES

All notices required or permitted under this Agreement shall be in writing and shall be deemed delivered when delivered in person or deposited in the United States mail, postage pre-paid, addressed as follows below. Either party may change such addresses from time to time by providing written notice to the other in the manner set forth below.

If for Client:

John Smith, Esq.
123 Main Street, Suite 100
Anytown, USA 12345

If for Consultant:

Rodney G. Richmond, RPh, MS, FASCP
The Mackenzie Group, Ltd.
Sherwood Lane, Glade Springs Village
Daniels, WV 25801

14. ENTIRE AGREEMENT

This Agreement, including *Appendix A (Fee Schedule and Payment Terms)*, contains the entire Agreement of the parties and there are no other promises or conditions in any other Agreement whether oral or written. This Agreement supersedes any prior written or oral Agreements between the parties.

15. AMENDMENT

This Agreement may be modified or amended if the amendment is made in writing and is signed and dated by both parties.

16. SEVERABILITY

If any provision of this Agreement shall be held to be invalid or unenforceable for any reason, the remaining provisions shall continue to be valid and enforceable. If a court finds that any provision of this Agreement is invalid or unenforceable, but that by limiting such provision it would become valid and enforceable, then such provision shall be deemed to be written, construed, and enforced as so limited.

17. WAIVER OF CONTRACTUAL RIGHT

The failure of either party to enforce any provision of this Agreement shall not be construed as a waiver or limitation of that party's right to subsequently enforce and compel strict compliance with every provision of this Agreement.

Client Initials: _____
Consultant Initials: _____

18. APPLICABLE LAW
    Laws of the State of West Virginia shall govern this Agreement.

19. VENUE
    The venue for the below signed Agreement is Raleigh County, West Virginia.

Party Receiving Services:

John Smith, Esq.
123 Main Street, Suite 100
Anytown, USA 12345
888-555-1212
By: _____
Title: _____Date:_____

Party Providing Services:

Rodney G. Richmond, RPh, MS, FASCP
The Mackenzie Group, Ltd.
Sherwood Lane, Glade Springs Village
Daniels, WV 25801
866-288-8386
By: _____
Title: _____Date:_____

Client Initials: _____
Consultant Initials: _____

APPENDIX A
FEE SCHEDULE AND PAYMENT TERMS

CONSULTING

Consulting time, including but not limited to, research, analysis, testing, inspection, review of materials, interviews, consultations, telephone conferences, report preparation, reading and correction of deposition transcript, review and signing of affidavits and similar documents will be billed at a rate of $250.00 per hour in five-minute increments plus expenses. Any time related to the case or project which is beyond the scope of an initial free consultation will be considered billable time. Reasonable estimates of time to be spent working on any aspect of the case may be provided upon request.

DEPOSITIONS AND COURTROOM TESTIMONY/APPEARANCES

Consulting at depositions, court appearances, or other legal testimony will be billed as follows: (1) Depositions or other legal testimony taken in my geographic area will be billed at $300.00 per hour at a minimum of four-hour increments; (2) Deposition, court appearances, or other legal testimony taken outside of my geographic area will be billed at a *per diem* rate of $3,000.00 per day plus expenses. For cancellation purposes, irrespective of geographic location, the billing rate shall be $500.00 per hour (See "Terms" section below). Billing is made for time being deposed, courtroom testimony, and waiting time. It is acknowledged that the Consultant will not be deposed or provide expert testimony if any invoices and/or retainer fees have not been paid prior to said depositions, court appearances, or other legal testimony.

EXPENSES

Consultant shall be entitled to reimbursement from Client for all out-of-pocket expenses including but not limited to lodging, meals, car rental, air fare, photography, audio/visual aids, materials, electronic research fees, laboratory fees, couriers, and specialized commercial services. A flat-rate administrative fee shall be applied per billing period for telephone including wireless and fax, and photocopying. Air travel shall be coach class, or the most cost-effective seating available; the Client will arrange and pay for this transportation at travel times convenient to the Consultant. Automobile mileage will be billed at the current IRS allowance. Estimates of expenses may be provided upon request.

TERMS

- A minimum retainer in the amount of $2,000.00 will be required prior to beginning work on new case assignments for un-established accounts, and will be held and applied to the last invoice. This retainer applies to work conducted in the geographic area of my office. See next paragraph for off-site/travel consulting.

- Prepayment of a retainer will be required for deposition, courtroom, or other legal testimony/appearance, based upon the estimated amount of time required to perform the function and the geography-specific rates quoted above, at least seven working days prior to the scheduled event. Time spent on such testimony/appearance shall be billed

Client Initials: _____
Consultant Initials: _____

against this retainer. Since such appearances may require travel to [client's state], all off-site consulting (meaning out of my home office geographic area) or court/deposition appearances will be included in the *per diem* rate.

- All invoices are due when rendered. Any credit balance remaining on the account from the retainer(s) after a case is completed will be refunded to the Client. Invoices 15 days past due will be charged interest at the rate of 1.5% per month (annual rate of 18%), and will be assessed a $200.00 late fee.

- Special tasks or areas of investigation might be recommended after initial evaluation of the assignment. Costs for and potential gains from such tasks will be discussed with the Client and will require approval before they are undertaken.

- Rates are subject to change. However, rates quoted at the time assignment is accepted will remain in effect for one year or until completion of assignment, whichever is earlier.

- Checks should be made payable to The Mackenzie Group, Ltd. (FEIN: xx-xxxxxxx).

Client Initials: _____

Consultant Initials: _____

Your initial conversation with the attorney and forwarding of your documents, e.g., *curriculum vitae*, fee schedule, and contracting agreement, are not billable time, but a cost of marketing your services. Nonetheless, beware of giving too much of your expert opinion at no charge in that initial conversation.

Fees for Time in Testimony

Testimony time for deposition, court, or arbitration hearings is usually charged in half-day or full-day increments, depending on the anticipated length of time. If the venue is local and the expected duration clearly is short, you can charge for a lesser period, perhaps two hours. Remember to include your travel time to and from, as you will be missing other work.

You should receive payment for time in testimony, either deposition or court, in advance. If you have made your requirements clear and have not been paid, do not begin your testimony until you are paid. This is not the time to be naive.

Requiring payment before scheduling your day out of the office is safer. One doctor ignored advice to require payment in advance and went to court to testify. The case settled on the courthouse steps, and he was not paid for the day away from his practice.

Another doctor was paid for one day's time in court testimony. At the end of the day, he was requested to appear a second day. The medical referral service that had obtained the engagement for him advised him not to show up until the attorney brought an additional check. He got the check. At the end of the second day, the same thing happened, and he received a check for the third day. His retaining attorney lost the case. Had he not stuck to the recommended policy, he quite possibly would have missed two days of work without compensation.

Deposition Fees

One notable expert, who charges $400 per hour for case review and court testimony time, charges $650 for deposition testimony time. He says that most abuse of the expert witness occurs in deposition, rather than in court in the judge's presence. He adds that the expert's engaging attorney does not always object when he should in deposition, because he hopes to settle and is therefore anxious to appear congenial.

In contrast, one surgeon says that he charges more for court testimony than deposition, due to greater stress. He feels pressure to "play to the jury" and also bears the weight of the case outcome, which may result largely from his testimony.

Although you may charge different rates for deposition and trial testimony, your rates should be the same for plaintiff or defense.

Importance of Advance Payment

Usually, opposing counsel will be paying for your time in deposition. This elevates the importance of being paid in advance for the anticipated period of time. If the deposition runs overtime, at the first appropriate point you should get the questioning attorney's agreement to pay, within a prescribed time limit, for the remainder of the time period. If you have made payment instructions clear and have arranged for adequate payment in advance, this will occur infrequently.

This issue should be discussed with your retaining counsel beforehand. He and opposing counsel should address payment and other points such as retaining counsel's having adequate time to cross-examine you. The bottom line to this issue is that your retaining attorney needs to work out the details in advance.

Videotaped Deposition Testimony

A number of experts charge more for videotaped deposition than live because of the stress of maintaining a constant visual presence. They feel that the effort to appear professional and stay completely on guard at all times for the camera merits a higher rate.

Expenses

An expert is not expected to absorb the expenses incurred in case preparation. If you decide to charge in itemized fashion for all expenses, both large and small, you may need to hire an accounting clerk. The time and effort required to accurately record every long-distance call, fax, photocopy, and postage stamp may negate the value of the money recouped. One expert who chooses not to nickel-and-dime the client simply adds a small amount of time to his billable hours to cover minor expenses incurred. Another charges a small flat-rate administrative fee for these expenses during each billing period. Certainly, major expenses such as travel and meals or photocopying whole file boxes of documents must be billed. The main thing is to clarify your policy up-front, in writing, so that there can be no misunderstanding.

It is preferable to have the client charge major expenses such as airfare and extensive hotel stays on his firm's credit card. If this is not possible and you have paid substantial reservation travel expenses, you should insist upon receiving reimbursement *before* leaving home.

A few experts add a handling fee, perhaps ten to fifteen percent, to the amount of expenses submitted. This practice encourages advance payment.

The most effective policy for expenses is to bill and collect reimbursement promptly and to arrange advance payment for large expenses. Do not get into the position of acting as the bank for the case.

Retainer

Charging an up-front retainer is prudent, particularly when dealing with an attorney or firm for the first time. Many experts recommend doing so on all cases. Many experts bill against the retainer, on the basis that after receiving a few payments they do not need a retainer. Others require that the retainer be replenished as soon as billings reach the amount of the retainer. Many require a retainer in place until the final billing.

Although not always possible, the ideal retainer would be enough to pay for all the time the expert expects to work on the case.

One expert recommends that an expert charge a substantial retainer to A) ensure that he is paid for initial work, B) assure him that he will most likely be paid for work assigned later in the life of the case, and C) make collections easier, because the attorney owes less money. He also suggests being flexible about the retainer, requiring a lesser amount from small firms.

Another valid reason for collecting a significant retainer is to cover the risk that you might pay for substantial expenses and then not be reimbursed or at least not in a timely fashion.

If the client writes the retainer check or if the law firm is small, inform them that you will not begin work until the check clears, unless you are given a cashier's check.

Although you may designate most of the retainer as refundable in case of settlement prior to expert work, you may want to specify a non-refundable portion. This covers the possibility that the attorney does not actually plan to employ you, but instead is retaining and naming you as the expert just so the other side cannot retain you. Another option is to require prepayment for specific services, such as IME and record review.

Wilma Couch, President of Med-Expertise, a respected medical referral service, advises, "Prior to giving any verbal or written report, if you have exhausted the retainer, stop and request additional payment." You have been forewarned.

Cancellations and Postponements

Doctors, particularly, need to set up a schedule of fee penalties for cancellations and postponements. A day in which no patients are seen is lost income. Determine how much notice you need to reschedule patients to fill your appointment calendar. Then set a sliding scale of how much of the advance payment you will need to keep to compensate for not being able to see patients. A few doctors charge a non-refundable administrative fee to set and hold the date.

BILLING PROCEDURES

Billing is usually done monthly. Still, there is no reason that you cannot bill more frequently, e.g., immediately after rendering service, and then at the end of the month simply review outstanding invoices and send statements. Frequent billing can prevent misunderstandings over how many hours are being spent, and helps avoids unpleasant surprises or claims of surprise.

A law firm's client may set a signing limit permitting the law firm to write a check only up to a certain amount. Bill frequently, rather than allowing the balance to become large. Frequency in billing is recommended when any third party is

FEE SCHEDULE

Detailed below is our current fee schedule. We have invested careful thought and consideration in preparing this based on our operational experience. Our foremost priority is to continue to provide timely, high quality professional services.

Document Packet – The purpose letter, complete medical records and X-ray films should be received in our office at least 10 calendar days prior to the date of service. Your presenting legible, well-organized records will facilitate the preparation of a high quality report. If disorganized records are received, there will be additional charges for our office to organize the records.

Late receipt of document packet	$ 50.00 per day (up to a $500 maximum)
Records organization	$ 50.00 per hour

Independent Medical Evaluation – Fee includes patient history and physical examination, a typed report, up to two (2) hours of document review of the materials delivered to us and up to a quarter (0.25) hour of phone conference time.

Prepayment (due one (1) calendar week in advance)	$ 1,000.00
Post payment	$ 1,100.00
Late payment (30 days or more after appointment)	$ 1,200.00
Cancellation less than three (3) working days in advance	$ 500.00
No-show fee	$ 500.00
Document review in excess of two (2) hours	$ 250.00 per hour
Supplemental reports	$ 250.00 per hour
Administrative time for follow-up to obtain documents	$ 30.00 per hour

Reports – Every effort will be made to provide a completed typed report within five (5) working days. If you will need a completed report more quickly than that, please notify us at the time the appointment is scheduled.

Accelerated report generation (to a maximum of $1,000.00 for "next day" report)	$ 200.00 per day

Document Review – There is a one (1) hour minimum charge.

Review	$	250.00 per hour
Written report	$	250.00
Supplemental reports	$	250.00 per hour
Administrative time for follow-up to obtain documents	$	30.00 per hour

Conferences – There is a 0.1 hour minimum charge. Services provided outside of our office are charged on a portal-to-portal basis.

Telephone conferences	$	250.00 per hour
Office conferences	$	250.00 per hour

Depositions and Arbitration Hearings – There is a one (1) hour minimum charge, which is prepaid as a non-refundable retainer applicable to date(s) rescheduled by the arbitrator/arbitration panel. Services provided outside of our office are charged on a portal-to-portal basis.

Deposition	$	500.00 per hour (one (1) hour minimum)
Arbitration hearing	$	500.00 per hour

Trial Testimony – There is a four (4) hour minimum. One (1) hour is prepaid as a non-refundable retainer applicable at the time testimony is scheduled. This retainer is applicable to date(s) rescheduled by the court. The remaining three (3) hours are prepaid and due five (5) business days prior to testimony. Services provided outside of our office are charged on a portal-to-portal basis. Travel time is included in the four (4) hour minimum.

Trial testimony	$	750.00 per hour (four (4) hour minimum)

Cancellations:

More than five (5) days in advance	All fees except the retainer are refundable or apply to the rescheduled date.
Fewer than five (5) but more than two (2) business days in advance	Half (50%) of the fees (except the non-refundable retainer) are refundable.
Fewer than two (2) full business days in advance	Fees are non-refundable.

involved, especially an insurance company. This policy is more critical if the client, not the attorney, is actually paying your bill, and is most common when the client is the defendant in the case.

To encourage fast payment when dealing with a government agency, offer a one or two percent discount if the bill is paid in full within ten days. One expert reports that some government agencies are required to take advantage of the discount.

Most consultants provide a time sheet showing the various tasks and time increments. Others maintain this record but do not provide this specific information with billing unless requested. They simply show the number of hours worked and general activities.

COLLECTIONS

Collections are best handled by a third party, even if just a friend. He can take a stance of reminding the debtor about the bill, stating that he is calling to make payment arrangements. This process keeps the image of the knowledge-based expert separate from the collection process. On the other hand, a letter sent from the expert can be a tactful reminder, clarifying and reminding the debtor of the arrangements.

The principal advice on collections is precautionary – work only for reliable clients, get as much money as possible in advance, and hold the retainer until the last invoice.

CONTINGENCY PAYMENT

Opposing counsel in a deposition or trial can make an issue of contingency payment arrangements. "Have you been paid? No? Then your payment depends on your testimony and the outcome of this case, is that correct?"

Put simply – do not do it. Such an arrangement for experts is illegal in certain states. At best, it is unethical. Agreeing to be paid on contingency calls into question the expert's objectivity.

ICF, Inc. • 123 Main Street • Anytown, USA 12345

XYZ Company, Inc.
123 Main Avenue
Another Town, USA 23456

Date

In reference to: Job Description

Account #xxx

Professional Services

			Hours	Amount
			#	$
Date	Emp.	Conference w/[company/contact] to discuss claims handling services and claims consulting/excess notices		
Date	Emp.	Document Review – [company/contact] Contract Review		
Date	Emp.	Claims/Loss Analysis – Excess Insurance Report		
	Emp.	Prepare Express Package		
	Emp.	Report Preparation – Copy Large Loss and excess reinsurance notifications		
Date	Emp.	Miscellaneous Clerical		

For Professional Services Rendered	00.00	$ 00.00

Additional Charges

		Amount
Date	Plane Fare – Claims Review	$
	Rent Car Expense – Claims Review	
	Tips – Claims Review	
	Hotel Charges – Claims Review	
Date	Auto Mileage – Consulting to [contact]	
	Parking – Consulting to [contact]	

Total Additional Charges	$ 00.00
Service Tax	$
Sales Tax	$
Total Amount of this Bill	$ 00.00
Previous Balance	$
Date Payment – Thank You	$ (00.00)
Balance Due	$ 00.00

Payments received after [month] 31st not shown on Statement.

PAYMENT DUE UPON RECEIPT.

[Company] Federal Tax ID #xx-xxxxxxx

TIME SHEET

Client _____ Consultant _____ Date _____

Client No. _____

TIME		REMARKS
	Telephone Conference with	
	Return Voice Mail	
	Conference with	
	Meeting with	
	Letter to	
	Fax to	
	E-mail to	
	Arrange Travel	
	Planning	
	Fact Gathering	
	Policy Review	
	Contract Review	
	Research	
	Misc. Clerical	
	Set Up Files, Filing	
	Prepare Express Package	
	New Client Files, Eng Notice, Filing	
	Account Supervision	
	Document Review	
	File Review	
	Deposition Review	
	Deposition Preparation	
	Trial Preparation	
	Deposition	
	Trial	
	Actuarial Analysis	
	Accounting/Data Entry	
	Report Delivery	
	Report Preparation	
	Exposure Survey	
	Retention/Captive	
	Underwriting/Rating	
	Claims/Loss Analysis	
	TOTAL	

REFERRAL AGENCY RATES

A referral agency might suggest that the expert reduce his fee so that the combined rate of the expert and the agency is not so high. This practice can create a credibility problem if attorneys know that you were willing to reduce your fee and therefore think that you should be willing to do so in other cases. Instead, create a higher combined fee with the agency so that *your* compensation remains consistent. This combined rate may make your rate noncompetitive, so you must weigh the risk of future credibility problems against the potential opportunity for immediate business.

THE ISSUE OF YOUR FEES DURING TESTIMONY

Opposing counsel may gasp dramatically in front of the jury members, many of whom make $10 per hour, and exclaim, "$200 an hour?"

Experienced expert Dan Poynter suggests a response such as, "My *company* charges $200 an hour, which pays for rent, lights, heat and other expenses, as well as my salary." If the attorney insists that you acknowledge that you are a sole proprietor, you can respond, "Yes, but my company still has overhead expenses."

Benjamin Cantor, J.D., legal photography expert, suggests a reply of, "I am being paid for my time, experience, expertise, and out-of-pocket expenses."

The attorney will also likely ask what percentage of your income is derived from forensic work. You need to know the number and be prepared to answer this question. Refusing to answer the question can incur sanctions, or penalties, placed on you by the court. When one medical expert is further questioned regarding the majority of his income coming from litigation support, he responds that he discovered that he really enjoyed the work and decided to devote more time to it.

Another, highly paid expert responds to an income percentage follow-up question, "Oh, that much?" with, "My field is very specialized and there are very few experts with as much experience as I have. After all, just like you, I only offer my time and my expertise." If the attorney then asks, "Doesn't that mean you're a professional expert witness?" the expert responds, "No, sir, I'm a professional (engineer, doctor, brick layer) who happens to have a forensic practice as a part of my overall professional activities."

If the attorney also asks the related question, "What percentage of your working time is devoted to this?," listen carefully to the question and answer appropriately. *Time devoted to forensic work* is different from *time devoted to testifying in court.* If the percentage of your working time devoted to forensic consulting is significant and you are asked, "Does that affect your opinion?" you can say, "No, in fact, the reason I am able to devote so much time (or am well-compensated) is that I give honest opinions. I can't last in this industry if I do not give honest opinions."

Regardless of the rates you charge, the court may consider your fee "unreasonable" for many different reasons and seek to reduce it. The primary reason this could happen is if the opposing side objects to your rate, which they are paying for deposing you. You should be ready, therefore, to justify the determination of your rate. This is also one of the reasons why your rate should be consistent.

COMMENT

Be poised and unapologetic about your income. You have paid your dues in your profession. If you are new to forensic work, I personally assure you that you will earn every dollar you are paid in the legal arena. Litigation support is always stimulating and challenging, occasionally inspiring, and potentially lucrative. It can also be stressful and perplexing and make you wonder whether justice can ever really be accomplished. Take pride in the fact that you are contributing to that goal and charge for your efforts.

CONTRACT

This IS Business

CHAPTER FOUR GUIDE

- The Need for a Contract
- The Documents
  - Terms of Agreement
- Agreement Signatures
- Indemnification
- Insurance

꘡꘡ Forensic work pays at a high rate, provides challenging work, sets no compulsory retirement age, and can possibly make you famous. Your appeal may even increase as you age. The major "fly in the ointment" experienced by experts seems to be the difficulty in collecting their fees from attorneys.

THE NEED FOR A CONTRACT

Not all experts have this problem. Why? Some work primarily with attorneys they know and a few are lucky, but most are diligent about doing the paperwork before they do the deal.

Sometimes experts hesitate to ask an attorney to sign an engagement letter or contract out of concern about possibly offending him. In truth, the attorney who scoffs at businesslike arrangements is much more likely to end the relationship in a decidedly non-businesslike manner. He may protest, after the work is done, that your rate is just too high and declare that he is going to pay you a lower rate. He may complain that you should have done the work in a shorter length of time. Or, he may decline to pay you at all.

Without an engagement letter or contract you have very little recourse. Experts relate little success in reporting such unethical treatment to the attorney's bar association. The option of suing the attorney is also a gamble. With a contract you should rarely experience a problem in collection and, in the event that you do, your chances of winning a dispute will be much greater.

THE DOCUMENTS

Some experts have a contract setting out the terms, a separate fee schedule, and an engagement letter. Others have a contract that contains a fee schedule and an engagement letter. Others combine all three functions into one document. Whatever form you use, get the agreement *signed* by the attorney or other person who retains you. When there is a dispute, insisting that you sent him a copy of your requirements will be useless if you then failed to get a signature agreeing to those requirements.

Terms of Agreement

Whatever contracting documents you choose to use, you need to include at least the following information:
- Fees
- Expenses Policy
- Retainer
- Billing Schedule
- Expected Payment Schedule

If you anticipate a problem with fee structure, ask the client to initial the rates.

State that all invoices must be paid up to date before reports will be delivered or testimony given.

You should outline payment arrangements such as the date an invoice becomes overdue and the penalty for overdue payments, such as a one and one-half percent charge on accounts not paid within 30 days. Verify that you are not in violation of usury laws. Late fees, on the other hand, can be substantial.

I am not convinced that charging interest on overdue invoices makes much difference in how quickly the invoice is paid. Nonetheless, the up-front statement of such a policy sets forth a business-like boundary of conduct.

Varying the fee for a service based on degree of promptness in payment may improve the timeliness of payment. In the illustration in Chapter 3, Orthopedic Surgeon Fee Schedule, Independent Medical Evaluation section, the fee for an IME evaluation ranges from $1,000 on a week's advance payment to $1,200 for payment 30 days or more after the appointment.

Include in your terms that any dispute over fees will be litigated in your jurisdiction, although even this policy has its pitfalls. If the debtor does not appear in court and you obtain a judgment, you must retain an attorney in his geographic area to handle the case and convince a court in his jurisdiction to recognize your court's judgment, and the debtor's assets must be located. To prepare for this last task in a worst-case scenario, a precautionary measure you might take is photocopying all checks you receive so that you have the bank routing numbers. As a matter of fact, copying all incoming checks is a sensible practice.

Insurance Consulting Firm Engagement Letter

Date

Attorney Name
Law Firm
Address1
Address2
City, State Zip

VIA FACSIMILE (555) 555-1234

Re: **Plaintiff v. Defendant, Court, Cause No.**

Dear **Attorney:**

We are pleased that ICF has been engaged to provide consulting services to **Law Firm** (client) in the above referenced matter. This letter describes the terms of that engagement. Once client signs this letter, this letter is a valid and binding obligation between ICF and client.

1. **Fees and Expenses:** ICF will charge fees for consulting services performed and its out-of-pocket expenses incurred in the course of this engagement. Fees will be computed on the basis of time actually expended by ICF's consultants and assistants and will be charged at ICF's standard hourly rates. A minimum of four hours will be billed on each engagement. Clerical time is

billed at $65 per hour. The ICF consultant that will be assisting you in this matter is **Consultant** (name). Fees for his time will be billed at his standard rate of **$$$$** per hour. At the end of each calendar month, ICF will promptly furnish client with an itemized monthly invoice of the fees and expenses charged, and when applicable, sales tax. Out of pocket expenses for travel, accommodations, meals, facsimiles, mail, long distance telephone calls, parking, taxis and car rental will be invoiced at cost. Mileage is billed at 36.5 cents per mile. Photocopies are billed at 20 cents per page. Our consultants fly first-class and do not bill for unproductive time spent while en route. If you would rather we fly coach we will do so but we will bill for all time spent en route, portal-to-portal.

2. **Cash Retainer:** Client has agreed to deposit with ICF concurrently with the execution of this engagement letter a **$5,000** cash retainer to be held until completion of the engagement. The cash retainer may, depending on the level or work involved, be increased or decreased from time to time by mutual agreement of client and ICF. The cash retainer will be returned at the client's request after all services have been billed by and paid to ICF.

3. **Payment Obligation:** Client will pay ICF in full promptly upon receipt of each monthly invoice for fees and out-of-pocket expenses. Client agrees that it is responsible for all fees and expenses incurred and ICF is not obligated to seek payment from any third party. ICF's invoices are due and payable at ICF's offices in (County), (State). Interest will accrue on all unpaid invoices beginning thirty (30) days from the invoice date at the rate of 18% per annum.

4. **Termination:** ICF reserves the right to terminate this agreement in event of non-payment of ICF's fees and expenses. ICF's consultants will not testify at deposition or trial and will not render any reports, declarations or affidavits if any invoices are past due. If any dispute arises concerning this engagement or ICF's fees and expenses, the parties agree that jurisdiction and venue over such dispute lies in (County), (State).

5. **Designated Representative:** Client designates **Attorney** (Name), as client's representative to communicate client's directions to ICF during the engagement hereunder.

If client has any questions concerning ICF's handling of any matter pursuant to the engagement discussed herein, please contact me. ICF will not begin work on this engagement until a signed copy of this engagement letter in addition to the cash retainer has been received by ICF. If this letter reflects client's understanding of the agreement between client and ICF under this letter, please indicate client's agreement by executing this letter in the spaces provided below and returning a copy of this letter to the undersigned. We are pleased to assist you in this matter and look forward to working with you.

Very truly yours,

_____

For ICF

Law Firm, Client

_____ Signature

By: **Attorney Name**

Its:

Agreed to and accepted

On _____, 2002

ICF RATE SCHEDULE

Associate	Service(s) Provided	Hourly Rate
Name	Executive/Consultant/ Expert Witness	$ 425
Name	Consultant/Expert Witness	$ 400
Name	Consultant/Expert Witness	$ 350
Name	Chief Actuary	$ 300
Name	Consultant/Expert Witness	$ 300
Name	Consultant	$ 300
Name	Consultant/Expert Witness	$ 295
Name	Consultant/Expert Witness	$ 285
Name	Consultant/Expert Witness	$ 275
Name	Consultant/Expert Witness	$ 250
Name	Consultant	$ 225
Name	Consultant	$ 200
Name	Actuary	$ 175
Name	Consultant/Expert Witness	$ 150
Name	Administration	$ 65

Exercise reasonable caution in the arrangement and execution of the contract documents. In the Chapter 3 example, Litigation Consulting Agreement of Rodney Richmond, every page is initialed to avoid page substitution or claims thereof.

While this chapter is primarily concerned with financial arrangements, the engagement documents should also address business issues. Include whether you are acting as a consulting expert or an expert witness, the scope of the assignment, what documents are being provided for your review, whether your opinion is to be oral or you are to prepare a written report, work schedules and deadlines, confidentiality, and return of records.

AGREEMENT SIGNATURES

Be clear about which party is your client. Are you working for the law firm or the client, such as an insurance company? The actual client, or responsible party, must sign the contract or letter of engagement. If, however, you work frequently for one client, e.g., a lawyer representing the same insurance company, requiring this documentation over and over might seem offensive.

Notice on the following engagement letter the requirement of signatures from both the law firm and the litigant. Also notice the security interest obligation to *secure* fee payment from any recovery (this is not contingency).

Financial Advisory Consulting Firm Engagement Letter

Date

Attorney
Law Firm
Address
Address

Dear Attorney:

RE: ABC vs. DEF

This letter is to confirm our understanding of the terms and objectives of our engagement pertaining to the above case.

We will act in the capacity of consultants in performing the services that you request of us on matters relevant to the financial concerns of the above-mentioned case, including investigative analyses and financial consulting services, as you deem necessary.

In addition, we will also be available, at your request, to testify as expert witnesses at deposition and/or trial.

Our services shall be confidential and we will not disclose information obtained pursuant to this engagement except at your direction or as required by lawful court order. All documents and records received will be controlled as to their access and availability. All such items will be returned to you or destroyed at your direction, upon the conclusion of our engagement.

The types and extent of our services will depend upon the nature of the case. Our services will consist of management advisory services and, therefore, will not contemplate the audit or review of financial statements. To the extent appropriate, we will independently verify those documents, transactions and records necessary to complete our tasks.

We have made no representations concerning the successful outcome of any contested claim or negotiation or the favorable outcome of any legal action for which we are providing services. We have not provided any legal advice to anyone related to this matter, nor are we in control of the preparation and/or management of any legal matters. All parties to this agreement understand that our involvement is limited to such actions as may legally be undertaken by this firm in its capacity of providing services in this engagement.

The fees for services rendered to you shall be based upon hourly rates, plus out-of-pocket costs for travel related expenses. The hourly rate charged will vary depending upon the level of staff performing the service. Our rates are as follows:

Principal-Senior Consultant	$325–550
Consultant	$225–350
Associate	$150–225
Staff	$75–150

The above rates are subject to change. New rates are effective from the date of change. Additionally, [Firm] does not charge for long distance telephone calls, facsimiles, copying or other administrative expenses. These costs are absorbed through a $4.00 per hour charge for each hour worked on the engagement.

In order to secure [Firm] in the payment of its fees, costs and expenses, the client agrees and does herewith deposit with [Firm] a retainer in the amount of $10,000.00, which shall be applied to the final billing from [Firm] to the client. At this time, we are unable to estimate our time and associated fees. As you know, fees may be greater or smaller depending on the cooperation of the parties and the level of effort required to complete the tasks required. All invoices are due and payable within thirty days. All amounts are due and payable before [Firm] employees will provide any testimony. If the invoices are not paid, we will cease all work until such invoices are paid. We understand that this engagement is in connection with litigation related to ABC and that we will ultimately look to ABC for payment of our fees.

If ABC becomes delinquent in its payment of fees and expense obligations to [Firm], we shall have the right to notify ABC, in writing, of our intent to terminate the employment and representation of ABC. The mere fact that ABC or [Law Firm] is unable to acquire substitute expert witnesses or litigation support in pending litigation is not grounds for prohibiting [Firm] from withdrawing from such engagement in the event that ABC becomes delinquent in the payment of its fee obligation.

If [Firm] is discharged by ABC or [Law Firm] prior to the conclusion of this representation, [Firm] is entitled to be compensated for its reasonable services, costs, expenses and disbursements. ABC's employment of [Firm] is at the will and discretion of ABC. [Firm]'s continued representation of ABC is at the will and discretion of [Firm]. However, if [Firm], in good faith, deems that it cannot provide support consistent with its legal and ethical obligations to its profession, or ABC persists in urging a position which [Firm] believes is not supportable based upon the information provided to [Firm] by ABC or by [Law Firm] and through the representation of ABC, then [Firm] may withdraw from further representation of ABC, return ABC's papers and files and ABC should then, in such event, seek other litigation support providers.

ABC represents that it is the full owner of the claims and matters for which it has engaged [Firm] and that ABC has full authority without encumbrance to prosecute same and to enter into this contract of employment.

[Firm] is granted a specific security interest in any recovery (whether it be money, property or otherwise) that may come to pass by compromise and settlement agreement, suit or judgment, to secure the payment of its fees. Further, ABC specifically agrees that in the event that any fees and/or unreimbursed expenses remain outstanding at the conclusion of representation hereunder, disbursement will be made directly from the recovery to [Firm] for all amounts due and owing prior to any disbursement of any recovery to ABC.

This agreement is binding on the parties hereto, their successors, executors, administrators and heirs and may not be altered or amended except in writing signed by all of the parties hereto.

THIS AGREEMENT AND ALL TRANSACTIONS CONTEMPLATED HEREBY, AS WELL AS ALL OF THE RIGHTS AND DUTIES OF THE PARTIES ARISING FROM OR RELATING IN ANY WAY TO THE SUBJECT MATTER OF THIS CONTRACT OR ANY TRANSACTION CONTEMPLATED HEREBY, AND THE ENTIRE RELATIONSHIP BETWEEN THE PARTIES, SHALL BE INTERPRETED AND CONSTRUED IN ACCORDANCE WITH AND THE ENFORCEMENT HEREOF SHALL BE GOVERNED BY THE LAWS OF THE STATE OF [XX] (WITHOUT REGARD TO ITS CONFLICT OF LAW RULES) AND ANY APPLICABLE FEDERAL LAW. IF ANY CONTROVERSY AND/OR LITIGATION BETWEEN ANY PARTIES SHALL ARISE, VENUE OF ANY LITIGATION AND/OR ARBITRATION SHALL LIE SOLELY AND EXCLUSIVELY IN [COUNTY, STATE], UNLESS MANDATORY VENUE RULES OR LAWS PROVIDE THAT VENUE MUST LIE IN ANOTHER COUNTY.

All claims and disputes of any nature relating to or arising under this agreement, any performance of duties relating to or arising under this agreement, any negotiations prior to the agreement, and any representations prior to or after the execution of this agreement shall be subject to arbitration in accordance with the applicable rules of the American Arbitration Association then existing. This arbitration agreement shall survive any execution of this agreement, any merger or integration clause, and shall continue to insure to the benefit of both parties hereto for all purposes. The parties hereto stipulate and agree that this agreement affects interstate commerce.

The person in charge of this engagement will be [Consultant]. Staff will be utilized during the engagement as the need arises. They will be assigned based on the experience level required to perform the work.

We have undertaken a review of our records to determine if [Firm] has conflicting professional relationships with the parties and entities involved in this case. No such relationships have been uncovered.

In accordance with [Firm] policy and investigatory accounting and expert witness work, it is mutually understood and agreed that our liability, if any, arising from services performed under the term of this engagement will not exceed the fees we have received for this engagement.

If the foregoing is in accordance with your understanding, please sign the copy of this letter in the space provided and return it along with the retainer check for $10,000.00 to us. We appreciate the opportunity to work with you.

Very truly yours,

[Consultant]

Accepted by: _____
                                [Law Firm]

Date: _____

Accepted by: _____
                                ABC

Date: _____

INDEMNIFICATION

I have seen disclaimers on expert witnesses' contracts stating that they will not be held responsible for this or that. Potential liability/risk management for expert witnesses is not within the scope of this book. I suggest that you consult an attorney (yours, not one who retains you for a case).

INSURANCE

Many experts are questioning the strength of judicial immunity to protect them and their assets. Several of the professional associations provide professional liability insurance coverage to their members. Not all insurance agents, however, understand forensic work. According to Jim Misselwitz, Insurance Consultant at

Evans, Conger, Broussard & McCrea, expert witness policies need to be tailored to reflect the need for professional coverage without relying on traditional coverage/event triggers such as bodily injury or direct property damage. Your policy should contain a definition of "expert witness" that accurately describes your professional activities.

CAUTION

Contracting documents are sufficiently complex to justify engaging an attorney – your own, not a litigation support client – to draft or edit and approve these documents. Note the points in the examples shown, and discuss them with your attorney. You do not wish to move from serving as an expert witness to being a plaintiff.

YOUR DATABASE

Your Most Valuable Business Asset

CHAPTER FIVE GUIDE

- Database Definitions
- Value of a Database
  - Mailing
  - Personal Contact
- Database Creation
- Database Records Construction
- Database Records Maintenance
- Database Improvement

꙱One of the most important parts of marketing strategy is building and maintaining a database of clients, prospects, and referral sources. In its most basic form, a "database" is a box of business cards, some with scribbled notes on them. At its best, a database is a computerized, detailed record of each person or business that includes contact data, personal information, relational experience, and a system of codes for sorting by various categories. The minimum data that an expert witness should have is an accurate listing of contact information such as names, addresses, and telephone numbers.

DATABASE DEFINITIONS

- *Database:* A list of contacts (individuals or firms) plus essential information about each, arranged in a logical manner, in which information is easy to retrieve and easy to use.
- *Record:* All of the information about one contact.
- *Field:* One element of information on the record, e.g., last name, category, date entered.

VALUE OF A DATABASE

The purpose of a database is to facilitate communication. The information in a good database is the core of your marketing. A database is necessary, in fact, essential, for mailing purposes, but is valuable in all areas of marketing.

Effective marketing consists of delivering the right message to the right prospects using the right methods. Your database should not only help you in determining the right prospects, but also furnish information to help you decide on alternative marketing and advertising methods. Consider the potential value of a refined list of groups such as, "A"-clients, "B"-prospects, "C"-people who can lead you to prospects, and "D"-people from whom you do not yet know what may come. Over time, especially if you enter more information than just contact data, the database starts to indicate such information as percentage of plaintiff versus defense lawyers, geographical concentrations, relative response from various mailings and other activities, frequency of contact, how many and what kind of contacts are necessary to secure an engagement, and a multitude of other factors. It becomes an essential tool in evaluating what you are doing right and what is not working effectively in your marketing efforts.

Assembling a mailing list of your own, with as much of this data as possible, is essential. Although you may occasionally want to rent specific mailing lists, e.g., all attorneys in your specialty from your state bar, for introductory mailings or one-time promotional projects the most effective promotion is consistent, multiple messages to the same people.

> ~ Your most important communications are to people with whom you have a relationship – even an insignificant one – or with whom you have a connection through other people. These are your best sources of business, and you must groom the goose that lays the golden eggs.

Mailing

Possessing a well-developed list encourages you to send regular mailings such as professional announcements of changes in your business, because the project is easy to do. A mailing does not seem nearly as formidable when you only have to compose the announcement.

Personal Contact

To get the maximum benefit from your list of clients, prospects, and referral sources, consider compiling the information in contact management software such as Act!,™ Microsoft® Access, or Goldmine.® Having an easily accessed electronic record with all the information about a client or prospect enables you to pick up the phone and make a contact easily.

Records in contact management software include fields for not only the mailing address and other contact information, but also for additional data about the individual or business. Such fields might include one that indicates whether the person is an attorney, a competitor, an associate, or other. One might indicate whether an attorney is plaintiff or defense. Another could indicate whether the individual is a client, prospect, or referral source. With these fields you can sort by category for mailings, and also search and find specific people or categories for a morning of making calls.

Make sure you keep a list of the codes you establish to use in the fields and what they signify, especially until you have worked with them for a while.

I recommend that you provide a large field in which to enter your observations and comments about the person, the relationship, or an event in which he was involved. Title the field "Experience" or "Comments." If you develop the habit of making notes in the record while talking to someone or immediately after the conversation, you will later find those notes quite helpful.

If you become proficient at using the software, you can click on a certain field, and a form letter that you have previously composed on word processing software will print out. For instance, if you have a standard follow-up letter, the name and address information would print out from the database, and the letter, with today's date, would print out from the word processing software. For a professional forensic practice this feature will not be used as often as it might in a standard business, but the option exists.

A field in which you enter the date that you wish to follow up with a certain individual can be very beneficial. As you contact people, enter comments about the conversation, and input an appropriate date in the follow-up field. Do the same when you send a letter. Then, each morning, enter the date or any date since you last worked in your contact records, using the Find function, and it will produce the first record with that date shown in the follow-up field. Repeat until you have worked all contacts scheduled for that day.

DATABASE CREATION

First, ask other expert witnesses whether they use contact management software and, if so, which kind and how the system has worked for them. Then choose software to buy, and arrange for help initially so that you do not become discouraged. Although the software is supposedly self-explanatory, most people need a little help in set-up. You can obtain assistance at a local computer store through classes, or they can help you hire an instructor to visit your office and walk you through the set-up process.

Once you have the forms set up for your database, input your clients. Then enter your best prospects, such as people who have inquired about your services. Enter your associates and people with whom you network and exchange favors. I recommend including your friends and family as well, as long as you code the records to indicate their categories. Mail your professional announcements to anyone who could possibly generate business or goodwill for you.

If you have not done so at this point, go through all the business cards you have accumulated, and enter the contacts in the database. If you have kept the person's business card, he probably belongs in your database, in one category or another.

Add "raw" prospects. A few experts have told me that they built their prospective client database by going through the Yellow Pages by hand. I suggest finding attorney lists on the Internet. They still have to be entered by hand, but the information is already organized. Remember to code a "raw" prospect differently from one with whom you have had contact. For example, if you title one field "Prospects," a "1" could designate a person with whom you have not yet had contact, a "2" a prospect to whom you have made an initial call, perhaps "3" a prospect to whom you have sent an introductory mailing, and so forth. Keep a record of what the numbers mean.

Database Record

Last Name		Date		Source	
First/Initial		Category	Code		
Hono					
Suffix		Newsletter			
Company		Comments			
Address 1					
Address 2					
City					
State					
ZIP					
Phone 1		Experience			
Phone 2					
Phone 3					
Phone 4					
Fax					
E-Mail		Follow-up Date		Action	
Web site					

After inputting a few people you might realize that your record form is not exactly as it needs to be to cover all the possibilities of categories needed, such as whether a person should receive your newsletter. Ask the software application professional from the computer store to come back, if necessary, and shift the category fields to reflect the data that you might have now realized will be most beneficial to you.

DATABASE RECORDS CONSTRUCTION

- Make the last name the first field on the record. This makes visually scanning through the records easier. When you pull the data for labels, you sort by category anyway.

  Enter the last name, the first/middle name, the honorific (honorary title such as Mr. or Ms.), if used, and the suffix (designation such as President or M.D.) all in separate fields.

  If you are not going to use the letter-writing capability but only the mailing label capability, you will not need to complete the honorific field in every record. Therefore, use the field mostly to designate Mr. or Ms. for gender-neutral names, such as Lee, Robin, Dale, or Leslie. Using the honorific field primarily for this purpose will make those few stand out, and can prevent awkwardness when talking to an individual on the phone. When you enter the data, you may not know the gender. When you find out, add it. Also, use the honorific field when you determine the gender of names from another language that do not indicate gender to you.

  Use Dr. in the honorific field if you do not know the doctor's designation. (Designations such as M.D. and PH.D. go in the Suffix field.)

  These recommendations about the honorific apply mostly for use in personal contact, as mailing labels customarily do not now require Mr. or Ms. When you run labels, go ahead and include the honorific in the query. On most of the labels the field will be blank, and a few will indicate Mr., Ms., or Dr., or an essential title such as Captain or The Honorable.

- Create a Suffix field for designations and titles such as JR., J.D., P.E., M.D., Executive Director, and President.
- Allow two fields for the address, e.g., one for the street name and number or post office box number, and another field for the suite, building, or apartment number.
- Use three separate fields for city, state, and zip code.
- Allow five fields for telephone numbers. In our increasingly connected world, having several numbers has become common. Label each field, indicating whether the number is a business, residence, pager, mobile, or fax number.
- Include fields for both e-mail and Web addresses.
- I recommend including a Source field. Use it to indicate the source of that name, e.g., a list or the name of the referring person. This information might come in handy.
- In addition to the fields you title with various categories you have chosen for data designation and sorting, include a couple of blank fields to accommodate your afterthoughts.
- Remember to code your competitors' records. As such, you will not want them to receive everything you mail.
- Protect yourself against your own possible errors. If necessary, ask for help in setting up certain fields so that they will not accept data other than correctly, e.g., the date as mm/dd/yyyy.

DATABASE RECORDS MAINTENANCE

The key to a database that enhances your business is to work on the records or have someone else do so, regularly, and I mean regularly. All the cards you customarily collect from meeting people should be checked against the database. If the information is not already in the database, enter it. If the information is in the database, verify its accuracy. As you receive mail from pertinent sources, compare the information against your database.

When you send a mailing that returns corrected information, input the valid data as soon as possible.

Be sure to collect e-mail addresses from business cards you receive and from incoming mail and e-mail. If in the future you wish to send a newsletter by e-mail you will appreciate your forethought.

There are services, such as the one at www.nationalchange-ofaddress.com, that can "clean" a mailing list, i.e., update the mailing address. I have not found using these services to be practical for a database that is more than simply a mailing list. Despite the company address still being valid, if the particular person on the list has left the company, the cleaning process might eliminate the listing. More importantly, in a contact database you should continually make notes to increase the value of the information for yourself. Such notes would include, e.g., meetings, conversations, and follow-up dates. A "cleaning" of a database substitutes the newly revised database for the old one submitted, and you would lose this valuable information. It is preferable to retain control by updating the mailing list by hand.

DATABASE IMPROVEMENT

Periodically assess your list. What additions do you need to make? Are there additional lists that you can buy or compile? Do you know non-competing experts with whom you could trade names?

Run queries by various categories and analyze the relative numbers. Is your database a reflection of your market? Do you need to reassess your target market? This kind of evaluation can be very useful in making marketing and advertising decisions.

Back up your database on a regular schedule and frequently on a diskette, a zip™ disk, or a CD. Alternate between two or three disks so that if one is defective, you are never too long past a good disk. Make this task part of a regular routine you do, such as weekly check writing. There is no way to comfort a person who has had a computer failure and lost massive amounts of data, most of which is irretrievable from other sources.

The first time you pull large numbers of records from your database to, e.g., create a disk to send to a mailing service, satisfy what might be justifiable paranoia. Back up your database right before you start; this will make you feel more secure. If your database has become large and therefore valuable, you might want to call the instructor you used from the computer store to pull the data for you, at least the first time.

C O M M E N T

If you are reading this chapter and saying to yourself, "Ho hum, mailing list; let's get to the important stuff," I urge you to rethink. You are in the communication business. Communication is the lifeblood of promotion. A well-built, well-maintained database is one of your most valuable business assets. Possibly you could even sell the information to a younger expert witness in your field when you retire. For now, your database is your field of prospects. The better you create and cultivate that field, the greater will be the crop you harvest.

BASIC BUSINESS COMMUNICATIONS

From Business Cards to Brochures

CHAPTER SIX GUIDE

- Business Cards
- Stationery
- Materials Upgrade
- Materials Timing
- Curriculum Vitae
- Photograph
- Brochures
  - Brochure Upgrade
  - Large Brochures
  - Most Popular Brochures
    - Content of the Brochure
    - Look of the Brochure
- Introductory Letter
- Inquiry Response Letter
- Your Personal Image for Deposition and Court
- Your Appearance Communicates
- Your Office Communicates

◡◡ This chapter focuses on visual communications, both printed materials and the image projected by the appearance of the expert. What does your appearance express about your knowledge of what is appropriate in a given situation? Does your image in court or deposition contribute to your success? Your printed materials represent you in your absence. What do they say about your professionalism, your thoroughness, and your attention to detail? These are questions to ask yourself as you assemble your basic communication tools.

BUSINESS CARDS

An effective business card tells who, what, and where. The information includes:
- Business name and individual name
- Type or description of business (called a tagline)
- Address
- Telephone numbers – local, toll-free, mobile, pager, and fax, all with area codes. (I have been shocked to see experts' cards that did not list their area codes.)
- E-mail address
- Web site address
- Optional logo

Choose carefully the description of what you do. That description, along with your name (and logo if you have one), constitutes your brand, the visual communication of your quality of service. Although legal marketing guidelines dictate conservatism, make the description work effectively for you.

State your specialty clearly and with the necessary detail to express what you do. Do not put only, e.g., "Litigation Support." All 200 people at the expert witness conference you will be attending do litigation support. How can you expect referrals from people if they do not know your particular specialty?

Certainly you can include a term such as "forensic," "litigation support," "legal case consulting," or even "expert," but *in addition* to your field of expertise. Although you may use the term "expert witness," I prefer one of the more acceptable terms mentioned above.

If your card indicates that you are a consultant, it is not imperative that you add a forensic term as well. If legal work is a major part of your business, however, I recommend doing so. If a medical doctor is not comfortable using terms such as "legal," "litigation," or "forensic," he may list only his specialty or add, e.g., Medical Case Review and/or IME. An alternative is to have a separate card for his legal and insurance work, different from the card for his clinical practice, as the example shows.

List your degrees and credentials. Health care professionals should certainly list, e.g., M.D., and, if appropriate, FA__ and Board Certified in ___, but do not get lengthy. When a prospective client follows up with you from having your card he will see all of your professional qualifications and affiliations on your *curriculum vitae.*

Placing your photograph on your card is acceptable, but do not do so at the cost of crowding information or making the print unacceptably small.

Creating a logo is not critical for an expert witness, although if used properly it can contribute to brand awareness. A symbol such as an oil derrick, the medical insignia, or an airplane provides instant recognition without requiring the design of a mark (logo), but is not necessary. Beware of cluttering your card.

An expert witness is usually an individual. If several people will be working together, compose a firm name, even if it is [Your Name] & Associates. A firm name can also denote what the firm does. If a firm name is used, your business card should also state your personal name. A card should not state two individuals' names, which requires that the reader of the card ask which one you are.

The Expert Witness Marketing Book

Bredemeyer & Associates, LLC
transportation consulting & litigation support

Ronald G. Bredemeyer, CFM/D

1102-A Petroleum Drive
Abilene, TX 79602-7955
E-mail: rbredemeye@aol.com

(915) 695-8809
Cell (915) 669-4424
Fax (915) 695-8974

JERRY H. WILLIAMS, P.E.

CONSULTING AND FORENSIC
ENGINEERING/CONSTRUCTION EXPERT
JWILLIAMS@JHWMSPE.COM

P.O. BOX 16227 • LAS CRUCES, NEW MEXICO 88004
TEL: 505.526.2444 • FAX: 505.526.0901
WWW.JHWMSPE.COM

Comprehensive Radiology Review, PLLC

A. Robert Tantleff, MD
Consulting and Litigation Services

57 Starling Court
East Hills, NY 11576

Voice: 516-626-2768
Fax: 516-626-6151
Email: artan@optonline.net

Since you are working in a serious, occasionally life-and-death field, your business card should be professional and low-key. Experts' cards should not be cute, odd-sized, or of unusual colors. Cards in white, beige, gray, or possibly a subdued blue color, with standard fonts look professional. As previously stated, the legal community is conservative, so it is in your best interest to conform. Most attorneys' cards, except ambulance chasers', provide good examples.

You may have been told that not only does an offbeat color make your card stand out, but an odd shape or a fold-over offers an advantage. I find that these are the ones that are most often thrown away. They do not fit into card file boxes, and they buckle when banded with others. The cost of creating business cards with slits at the bottom to fit onto Rolodex® card file holders is debatable. I have not seen such a system sitting on anyone's desk in a long time, and this kind of card does not fit in a box of standard cut cards.

An exception is that many journalists use a Rolodex.® In a publicity media kit, for the few experts who would ever use one, a Rolodex® card should be included.

Make the print a reasonable size. If a middle-aged person has to get out their drugstore glasses just to read the name on your card when they meet you, the print is too small. Remember that baby boomer attorneys are the ones leading the pack!

Put thought into the design of your card, but paying a design artist is not absolutely necessary if your budget is limited. Study attorneys' cards and select appropriate font styles and print size from your printer's books.

STATIONERY

Like business cards, stationery should be dignified and professional looking. It is often a prospect's first impression of you and should be designed accordingly. Use letter-sized paper, which indicates business professional, unlike personal, note-size stationery. Standard attorney colors, such as white, beige, gray, and perhaps blue, are preferable. With discretion you can add a bit of color with the letterhead ink. For instance, maroon looks good on gray paper. (You would not type your letters with maroon ink; always use black for the letter itself.) In the letterhead do not use excessively scrolled script, which is attractive but more difficult to read than straight font. Envelopes should be number ten, not under-sized or card-sized.

Collect samples of attorneys' stationery and fashion yours in a similar style. Along with your business cards, you can design your stationery and have it printed inexpensively at your local print shop.

MATERIALS UPGRADE

〜 Although business cards and stationery can be acquired on a modest budget, having them professionally created at the beginning of your practice is optimal. A graphic designer can design a distinctive look, a signature to carry through on all of your materials. The elements of that look, or brand, are your business name and tagline, or description, with or without a logo. A customized look is built by careful selection and use of type, layout, and color.

My graphic designer, Cynthia Pinsonnault, suggests, "Make your materials look like you would look if you were going into the bank to borrow a million dollars."

Obtaining professional assistance sooner rather than later (when you have already distributed materials) is preferable in fashioning an attractive, *consistent* style, to create brand identity.

MATERIALS TIMING

If you plan to create a Web site within a short time, reserve the domain name and list the address on all of your business materials, along with your contact numbers and e-mail address.

CURRICULUM VITAE

Most people desiring to build an expert witness consultancy are professionals who already have a *curriculum vitae*, or resume. You may also choose to compose a short version of your *c.v.* for use in a publication, on the Internet, or as a direct mail piece. Title the short version something like Brief Bio or Biographical Sketch to avoid troublesome questions about having more than one version of your *c.v.* NOTE: *Do not compose one* c.v. *for plaintiff and a different* c.v. *for defense.*

To update your resume for use with attorneys, verify that you have included all the points of education, licenses and certifications, continuing education, and experience that support the areas of expertise in which you are qualified to testify.

Do not give unnecessary or private information, such as your birth date, Social Security number, marital status, or hobbies. Delete irrelevant associations such as your homeowners' group. Exercise caution. If you work in criminal cases or even emotionally charged areas such as Workers' Compensation, do not publish your home address and home telephone number.

Be certain to list all necessary contact information.

Review the information carefully for content.

Look over the resume again, this time without actually reading the information, looking for "sense of flow" of the information. Do the section titles really indicate their content? Is the information easy to follow from one page to the next? Can you tell what page you are reading at any point?

Then scan the pages for appearance. Glance over them for overall look without reading the information. Are the margins straight? Are the indentions consistent?

Ann E. Reisch, CCIM, CPM, RPA
Premises Liability and Property Management Expert

Reisch Consulting Group, Inc.
2316 Chinook Trail, Suite 110
Maitland, Florida 32751

Phone: (407) 628-2742   Fax: (407) 628-2561
E-mail: aereisch@aol.com

Areas of Expertise:	Experienced in managing all types of commercial properties in addition to the management and leasing of residential properties.
	Premises Liability
	Commercial Property Maintenance
	Standards of Care
	Management Practices, Policies and Procedures
	Slips, Trips & Falls
	Inadequate Security
	Negligent Hiring, Retention & Supervision
	Management Company Operations
	Landlord Tenant Disputes
	Lease Interpretation/Administration
	Expense Calculations & Reconciliations
Education:	B.S. Business Administration
	Illinois State University
Professional Qualifications:	Licensed Real Estate Broker – State of Florida
	Certified Commercial Investment Member (CCIM)
	Certified Property Manager (CPM)
	Real Property Administrator (RPA)

Professional Experience:	President – Reisch Consulting Group, Inc.
	Senior Vice President Property Management – Realty Capital TCN / Worldwide
	Director of Property and Facility Management – Lincoln Property Company
	Property Manager – Heitman Properties, Ltd.
	Property Manager – Trammell Crow Company
Awards:	Certified Property Manager of the Year Institute of Real Estate Management
Professional Affiliations:	Institute of Real Estate Management
	CCIM Institute
	National Association of Realtors
	Florida Association of Realtors
	Orlando Regional Realtor Association

Is the font easy to read? Are the font style and type size of the section titles consistent?

Check for grammar, punctuation, and spelling.

Consistency of punctuation is more critical than choice of style, such as whether book titles are in italics or within quotation marks. Make certain that all book titles are treated identically, and the same for journals, periodicals, radio and television show titles – all the items in one category punctuated the same.

Ask at least two other people to proofread your resume.

After all corrections and changes have been made, verify once more that you have not left out essential information and also for accuracy of data. Check specifics, especially dates, over and over. A harmless error could be pounced upon and used by opposing counsel to make you look careless or, worse, dishonest.

Review a last time for appearance, spelling, and punctuation.

PHOTOGRAPH

Adding your photograph to your resume is beneficial. No conscientious attorney would engage an expert for testimony without knowing what he looks like. A professional photo should be a head shot, cropped just below the tie knot or neckline. Although not essential, color looks good and may not cost much more than black-and-white.

Spend the money to use a photographer who works with professionals, not just babies and families. He will make you look better and more credible than you think you are. He will create a contact sheet containing many shots. Get assistance in selecting the one that looks the most professional, intelligent, and trustworthy.

You can simply enclose your photo with your resume, without going to the trouble of printing it on the resume. Keeping them separate makes using a color photo easier. Companies that copy photos for models will make multiple 5×7 copies inexpensively. This is the size preferred by the media for publicity purposes, but wallet-sized will do as well for attorneys. Take the contact sheet from the photographer to the photo copy service, with the selected photo marked. They can help you decide how to crop the photo.

BROCHURES

The primary purpose for a brochure is to present expertise and services. Having a brochure is not absolutely essential, particularly for an individual. For either an introductory mailing or when responding to a request for information, an individual can simply enclose an abbreviated *c.v.* and a business card with a cover letter. Furthermore, if you are a sole practitioner and you are especially sensitive to the question of whether traditional advertising is appropriate for your forensic consulting practice, do not feel compelled to use a brochure.

One reason an individual might want a brochure, similar to a company brochure, is that he can state his areas of expertise and the services he offers as well as his background. There are experts who feel that a *c.v.* should follow an academic rather than business format, including only items such as education, licenses and certifications, experience, and publications and presentations. Conversely, the opinion of an attorney with whom I consulted regarding this issue was that attorneys want as much information as possible about the expert and are not offended by a *c.v.* that does not follow a strictly academic format.

For a firm of experts, a brochure is essential to communicate the experts' various qualifications and services, in introductory mailings and response letters, and as a piece to be handed out.

You can create a simple brochure and either produce it on your PC or have it professionally printed at a reasonable rate. For a large, folder-type brochure that may contain additional promotional items (often called a portfolio), you will probably want professional help. For either, a money-saving idea is to contact an art school or a local college to see whether an intern could do your work at low or no cost. The instructor might use your brochure as a class project. If so, you could end up with several different ideas from various students – viewpoints that you might not have considered.

Brochure Upgrade

Although having a professional designer create your brochure is a budget consideration, the difference in quality can be worth the investment.

If you use a professional, I recommend that you look at his portfolio of previous work. It could reflect a personality so different from your project that you might decide to shop for a different designer.

Brochure (Actual size flat = 8 × 9 Inches)

A small 4-panel brochure measuring 4 inches by 9 inches, when folded, can fit into a #10 business envelope or, like this example, can be printed as a self-mailer.

ATTORNEYS AND MANAGERS need a reliable partner to provide environmental and regulatory knowledge, focused scientific analysis and application of leading-edge technology. SSCI addresses our clients' needs by providing a wealth of scientific and business expertise coupled with advanced information management and graphical presentation capabilities.

SEPARATION SYSTEMS CONSULTANTS, INC. (SSCI) has assembled a highly diverse and talented team to provide technically-correct solutions for clients with an emphasis on quality, budget and schedule.

SSCI'S CONSULTATION and support services are designed to provide our clients with a distinct advantage based on sound scientific principles and intelligent use of persuasive presentation materials.

Corporate Office
17041 El Camino Real, Suite 200
Houston, Texas 77058
281-486-1943 • Fax: 281-486-7415

Nationwide
1-800-324-7724

Austin **Dallas** **Louisiana**
512/990-5799 214-890-4029 504-876-4080

ssci@sscienvironmental.com

www.sscienvironmental.com

Environmental Consultation and Litigation Support

SSCI PROVIDES A FULL complement of environmental consultation services including technical support, technical analysis of case merits and strategic planning.

Technical Consultation
• Affected property assessments
• Hydrogeology, chemistry and toxicology
• Exposure and risk assessment (human and ecological)
• Fate and transport modeling (air, soil, groundwater)
• Financial analysis and cost estimation
• Remediation design and evaluation

Program Expertise
• RCRA/CERCLA/TRRP/RECAP
• Voluntary cleanup and innocent owner/operator programs
• Environmental site assessments and real estate transactions
• Permits and compliance plans
• Petroleum storage tanks
• Wetlands delineations and ecologic studies

Management Support
• Coordination of workflow between expert witnesses and attorneys
• Management of quality, budget and schedule for litigation team
• Technical support of expert witnesses

Research and Analysis Support
• Data validation
• Literature and database searches
• Scientific review and critique of depositions and documents
• Analysis of existing case data and design of supplemental studies

Document and Information Management
• Electronic management of transcripts and evidentiary documents
• Customized database development and support
• Scanning, OCR and document libraries on CD-ROM

Graphics Support
• Preparation of multimedia courtroom graphics
• Advanced CAD mapping and computer graphics presentation

Large Brochures

These are costly to produce and costly to mail. If you create and use a large brochure, do not waste them in first-approach direct mail campaigns. Save them for response mailings to prospects who have expressed interest and requested additional information.

Large brochures come in many varieties – bound, booklet, or loose pages in a folder or portfolio. The advantages of using loose pages in a folder are that the information can be easily updated, and that you can arrange the pages in a different order for different clients. The disadvantage of loose sheets is that they can become rearranged and even misplaced by the recipient.

The benefit of a large brochure or portfolio is that more information can be included, such as extensive biographies of the principals, photographs, charts, diagrams, letters of recommendation, and lists of previous cases.

Most Popular Brochures

A less costly brochure is most often a sheet $8\frac{1}{2} \times 11$ inches or slightly larger, with text on both sides, folded twice to become approximately $\frac{1}{3}$ the size of a sheet of paper. The stock should be thicker than printer paper, but thin enough to fold without crimping.

The brochure should read from left to right in columns when unfolded horizontally. The words are hard to read in the folds when the text moves across two or three panels. Instead, arrange the text independently in each panel, although the content can continue from the bottom of one panel to the top of the next panel. Organize the panels for a logical flow of information – beginning on the outside front panel, move to the inside left, then to the middle and to the right, and then to the remaining two panels on the back. One back panel can be left blank except for your return address, so that the brochure becomes a self-mailer, or you can use all of the space for text.

A possible arrangement of elements on one of the panels is to have either a headline or your company name positioned at the top of the panel, so it can be seen when sticking out of a breast pocket.

Another nice look for a brochure is a sheet 7½ inches tall, folded once, so that the piece ends up with four panels instead of six.

You can cut a slot to hold a business card, but this adds cost. You can even create pockets in a brochure to hold replaceable insertions of information, similar to those frequently seen in large kits.

Content of the Brochure

The brochure needs to contain your biographical information – your education and professional experience, qualifications, affiliations, credentials, and honors from your resume. You can also list a few of your published writings. Hit the high points, but, again, save the long form for your *c.v.*

﹏ A brochure does not have to tell everything there is to know about you or your firm; it is, instead, an invitation to communicate further.

The text should include a complete description of your area of expertise and the services you are able to perform for attorneys. You might include a reference to one or more well-known cases in which you have been involved, but do so with caution. Get permission from the attorney.

Do not put your rates in your brochure. Financial arrangements are factors that are best discussed in follow-up communication.

Your brochure is a good place to cite positive comments that clients have made about your services. The word "Testimonials" is a little shop-worn; try "Success Stories" or "Client Comments."

As with citing cases, be cautious about using a name without the person's permission.

Photos can make a brochure eye-catching. Consider using not only your personal photo, but also photos of objects or scenes pertaining to your field of specialty. Studies show that readers' eyes are drawn first to photos. If you use a side-view photo of a face, position the photo so that the eyes look inward to the page, rather than outward toward the edge of the page.

Although this should be obvious, experience has proven otherwise – *Make certain that the brochure clearly indicates how to contact you.*

Triple-check for accuracy and spelling. Be brief and interesting. Do not be overly boastful, though you are allowed to use descriptive phrases such as "award-winning," "honored in the …," and "recognized by the …" if they are factual. Use correct grammar. Beware of using inner-circle language or abbreviations that people outside your industry would not understand.

Look of the Brochure

As with all advertising, leave white space. Do not fill every inch and line. What you say will more likely be read if there is adequate space throughout the text and particularly around the outer edges of the page to direct the reader's eye to the text.

After you have decided what you want to say and include, a designer can help you arrange the text and graphics attractively and effectively. He can also advise you on currently popular fonts. A conservative look does not have to be an outdated look. With desktop publishing making it possible for designers to work independently, graphics design has become relatively inexpensive.

Do not let yourself be overly influenced by excessively artistic designers; this is a communication piece, not a work of art. Four-color printing may be essential to how you want your brochure to look, but then again it may not. For instance, printing the body of the brochure in black, then judiciously using one spot color for emphasis can be visually appealing and cost-effective. Study other people's brochures and you will begin to form an opinion of your own, similar to studying art.

INTRODUCTORY LETTER

The most important points to include in an introductory, or solicitation, letter are the subject line and the P.S. (postscript).

The attorneys who will read your letter bill their time by the hour. They condition themselves to scan for main points and skip the prose when they are not working on billable time (and probably even when they are). To increase the odds of the letter being read, the subject or reference line should indicate the topic of the letter, e.g., Environmental Litigation Expert or Earning Capacity Studies.

The letter should be direct and succinct and, preferably, not more than three short paragraphs on one page. The first paragraph introduces you and why you are contacting the recipient, and the second states the benefits of using your services, usually including the quality of your credentials. The third closes with a friendly request that the reader call for more information, engage your services, or keep your information on file for future use. Marketing jargon calls these three points bait, argument, and call to action.

The "bait" does not have to be as clever as it might for a letter aimed at creating a need rather than filling one that already exists (attorneys know they need expert witnesses). You can make the first sentence somewhat provocative: *"Claims in the area of ___ are increasing daily! As a ___ I can offer competent and comprehensive assistance in the following areas:"* or moderate: *"As a clinical pharmacist I understand the challenges you face in clarifying issues associated with drug-related injuries and*

Project Support Group, LLC

Date

Mr.
Firm
Address

RE: Construction Project Management Expertise

Dear Mr. [attorney]:

I would like to offer my services to your firm as a construction litigation consultant and, if necessary, for expert witness testimony.

My company, Project Support Group, has developed a computerized management system, Retriever II,™ which allows the attorney to view all of the pertinent data in a logical framework and to present with accuracy and credibility the facts supporting the claim. Our unique relational database capability is enhanced by my thirty years' experience in project management, contract administration, CPM scheduling, claim preparation and dispute resolution. I have testified before State Courts, the Federal Court of Claims and Arbitration Panels.

Enclosed are my *c.v.* and a brochure detailing our services in construction litigation matters. I would be happy to be of service to you in this matter. Please call me at your earliest convenience.

Sincerely,

Robert J. Dacre
Consultant

P.S. We specialize in identifying and providing evidence as to who did what and when.

3665 Frederick Drive, Ann Arbor, MI 48105
Phone: 734-663-8015 • Fax: 734-668-1795
www.projectsupportgroup.com

adverse outcomes," or merely state that you are sending your materials for his possible use.

In the example shown, I took a conservative approach. Construction attorneys already know that data management is the critical factor in litigating complex construction cases. Therefore, the problem the attorney needs for an expert witness to solve in construction litigation can be presented in the "argument," the body of the letter, rather than the first paragraph.

Do not forget to ask for the business. Do not appear desperate or overly eager but, certainly, interested.

Add a P.S. that will lodge in the reader's mind – "You can always find my information on JurisPro.com," "One of few vocational rehabilitation experts with Assistive Technology Expertise."

As discussed in the chapter on direct mail, the letter is accompanied by either a *c.v.* or a shorter biographical sketch, and a business card. (Most experts' *c.v.*'s are lengthy and therefore it is too costly to include them in initial solicitation mailings, and an attorney would not take time to read a long *c.v.* unless he were already interested.)

INQUIRY RESPONSE LETTER

A letter in response to an inquiry will be longer by its nature. Content will be dictated by the complexity of the services you offer, as well as the details required to respond to the attorney's description of the case. Nonetheless, stick to the point. If you are needlessly wordy, the attorney can assume you will rack up unnecessary consulting time and/or bore the jury. This letter might secure the engagement, so you must promote the benefits of your services in the best light. If your services involve multiple functions to be performed, feel free to enclose a separate list.

This is the appropriate communication in which to cite previous consulting and testimony and statements of client satisfaction, attributable if possible.

Include your fee schedule and retainer requirements with the letter. You may include an engagement contract just for information and certainly do so if you expect to be retained when this information is received.

Bear in mind that you are not yet engaged and, most likely, others are being evaluated as well. So put your best foot forward. But *do* ask for the job, in a professional manner.

CAUTION

Do not give opposing counsel fodder with which to impeach your testimony based on breach of objectivity. For instance, in introductory or response letters do not say something like, "I can help your side win." Be more creative and less crass. Be subtle but clever. Do not compose different letters for plaintiff and defense, either solicitation or response.

YOUR PERSONAL IMAGE FOR DEPOSITION AND COURT

All of us like to be with people similar to ourselves. We feel comfortable and at ease. A safe position is to dress like an attorney, but not necessarily expensively, and certainly not in a manner as flashy as some do. The key word is conservative. A medium or dark blue, brown, or gray suit is always appropriate. Jury consultants tell us that juries consider a blue suit a sign of showing respect for the court. This attitude probably comes from our cultural history, when most people did manual labor and had only one dress-up outfit. For men that attire was a navy blue suit, which they wore to weddings, funerals, and court.

Wear a solid color shirt or blouse. If you will be videotaped, choose light blue, as white can reflect light onto your face. Your tie or scarf should be simple.

Wear a minimum of jewelry, two pieces at most. Bracelets and large cuff links can make distracting noise on a tabletop or near a microphone.

The Expert Witness Marketing Book

Do not wear lapel pins, rings, or necklaces that indicate your religion, academic honors, or other achievements and affiliations.

Remove excessive coins from your pockets. Do not carry bulky items that distort the smooth line of your pants.

Do not wear sunglasses inside nor, preferably, even light-sensitive glasses, which also can make your eyes unreadable to a jury. Do not rest your sunglasses upon your head.

For deposition and court appearances always research regional expectations. Do not assume. For example, we Texans are amused that a few people from other regions still think that we all wear jeans, drive pickups, and carry guns. In actual practice, court in Texas is a formal affair. A participant might on occasion wear cowboy boots, but they will be dress boots, not work boots, and they will be shined. Above those boots will be a suit. Etiquette demands that a gentleman's hat, even a cowboy hat, be removed when indoors.

Individual customs prevail in other regions as well. Be cautious of wearing too casual academic wear, such as "earthy" shoes. When you do not know the custom, adhere to conservative and slightly formal attire. Imitate attorneys' style of dress. To reiterate, your appearance should be a non-issue. How you look for court should be a matter for neither admiration nor criticism.

YOUR APPEARANCE COMMUNICATES

The above suggestions, although primarily applicable for deposition and court appearances, also apply to your image when personally marketing yourself to attorneys. The objective is to make your appearance so conservative and professional that nothing about you distracts from your message. When networking with an attorney or attending an interview for possible engagement, you want his confidence in your appearance to be a foregone conclusion once he has met you. Many attorneys will not use experts they have never met, because appearance before the jury is so critical.

An expert in truck driver training is often requested by the retaining attorney to wear to court a sport shirt and washable pants, clothes he wears when working. The attorney you represent may make similar requests. Nonetheless, for your initial meeting with the attorney, always wear a suit; it is the legal team uniform.

YOUR OFFICE COMMUNICATES

Most experts' offices, especially home offices, are rarely seen by their attorney clients. If you invite clients to your office, it must certainly be clean and professional and contribute to the image you want to convey.

Effective, courteous telephone communication is critical. The phone must never ring unanswered. A person, a service, or a recording must answer your phone, or you are wasting your time and money soliciting business. Telephone courtesy (and a desire for business) dictates that a phone be answered by the third ring.

Investigate periodically how your associates, employees, family members, answering machine, or answering service handles your calls when you are out of the office. Have a friend call, pretending to be an attorney, and make notes of how quickly the call is answered, the tone of voice he hears, and the professionalism with which he is treated. Then also notice how quickly you receive the message.

～ Trite, but true – You never get a second chance to make a good first impression.

The Expert Witness Marketing Book

NETWORKING

The Key to Your Success

CHAPTER SEVEN GUIDE

- Inform Your Immediate Circle
- Create Referrals from Your Peers
- Build Relationships with Other Expert Witnesses
- Trade Business with Your Competitors
- ASK for Referrals
- Send Thank-You Notes
- Network with Attorneys
  - Show Your Communication Skills
  - Convey Your Attitude
- Go Where the Attorneys Are
  - Attend Attorney Group Meetings
  - Attend CLE Classes on Your Subject of Expertise
  - Teach CLE Classes for Attorneys
  - Socialize with Attorneys at Judicial Fundraisers
  - Contribute to and Attend Attorneys' Charity Events
  - Meet Attorneys Speaking at Expert Witness Conferences
  - Become Involved with Law Schools in Your Area
  - Exhibit at State Bar and Trial Attorney Association Conventions
- Networking Skills
  - Practice Your Statement of Profession
    - Examples of Statement of Profession
    - Unique Selling Proposition
  - Adopt a Networking Mentality
  - Do Not Be Reticent
- Communication Skills
  - Be Interested, Not Interesting
  - Nametags – a "Little Thing"
- Stay in Touch

The Expert Witness Marketing Book

A referral from one attorney to another attorney is the most popular method of finding an expert, as indicated by the Reader Profile Study from *Lawyers Weekly USA*. Although this study is three years old and Internet search has continued to increase in popularity, referral is still consistently the top method.

Reader Profile Study 1999 and 1994, Harvey Research, Inc. for *Lawyers Weekly USA*

If a matter arises in which you need an expert witness, how will you locate one?	1999	1994
Ask a fellow attorney for a referral	78%	77%
Consult legal publications for advertising	32%	41%
Search an expert directory on the Internet	30%	9%
Look through the Yellow Pages	5%	7%

People feel more confident and comfortable with people they know or with people introduced to them by people they know. Commit to developing your networking skills and building a referral network. The payoff will be well worth the effort.

INFORM YOUR IMMEDIATE CIRCLE

Ensure that your accountant, banker and other service professionals know that you are available for litigation consulting. Tell your family and friends what you do; they will probably find legal work fascinating, and almost everyone knows someone in the legal profession. In speaking to a person who is not an attorney, keep your statement simple and use commonly understood terminology whenever possible.

CREATE REFERRALS FROM YOUR PEERS

At your trade or professional meetings, inform your peers that you are engaged in litigation support. On occasion an attorney will simply locate a person in a particular line of work and ask him to consult on a case, and many of them will decline. You want your associates to recall that you do litigation consulting and refer attorney calls to you. An interesting conversation opener at a meeting is, "Have you ever been contacted by an attorney to consult on a case?"

When you receive a referral, record the details – not only the contact information of both the referring person and the one to whom you are being referred, but also their relationship and any pertinent details, even personal ones, such as their families' annual ski trip together. Write down the information and keep the two people connected in your mind, perhaps by writing on the back of the business card of the person to whom you are talking. You will want to record this information in your database when you return to your office. Be sure you have permission from the referring person to use his name when contacting the other person.

BUILD RELATIONSHIPS WITH OTHER EXPERT WITNESSES

Mix and mingle at forensic conferences. Attorneys will often ask an expert if he knows of an expert in another field, especially if the fields are related. Assess the other areas of expertise used in your cases, and build relationships with experts in those fields. For instance, a personal injury case might require a doctor, a vocationologist and/or economist, and possibly a physical therapist. A premises liability case might require a forensic crime lab analyst in addition to a security expert. In your database of clients, prospects, referral sources, friends, and associates, also include experts, both in your field and in others. Expert witnesses comprise a relatively small field. Become acquainted with as many people as possible, and develop strategic alliances.

TRADE BUSINESS WITH YOUR COMPETITORS

Each of us is unique in how our personality, education, and professional and life experiences have shaped us. As a result, we do not have much actual head-to-head competition. No one else knows exactly what you know. No one else has experienced what you have. Certainly, no one else explains the same set of facts exactly as you do. I believe that a healthy attitude of regarding supposed "competitors" as quasi-associates will benefit you in several ways.

Think of your prospective clients as a large and ever expanding pie, of which there are plenty of slices for everyone. Fortunately and unfortunately, there is a plethora of litigation. This viewpoint should prevent you from feeling, sounding, and acting desperate. Another case is always out there.

When you cannot accept a case because of a disagreement with the premise or a conflict with the attorney, litigant, or schedule, consider referring the case to another expert in your field. The attorney will remember your helpfulness and openness, and the associate will owe you. Contact the expert and let him know that you sent one his way. By the law of reciprocation, it is likely that in the future he will send you a case (or two) in return.

Do not wait for an associate to refer business to you and then reciprocate. Cast your bread upon the waters. Give and it shall be given unto you. Trite? Perhaps. But true. One principle of networking is to look for ways to help as many people as you can, regardless of whether or how they can help you. As stated by Ralph Waldo Emerson in his essay entitled, "Compensation," the longer you put in without getting out, the better your result when it finally comes. It is a truism that you can have anything you want in life as long as you help others get what they want. The goodwill is certain to come back to you.

Another time you really *should* refer a case to an associate is when you are asked to consult and possibly testify in an area or subtopic of your profession in which you are not totally competent. Again, let the expert whom you referred know of your good deed.

Never allow yourself to feel that you "must have" any one case, client, or relationship. Besides the breach of integrity, you could be crucified on the stand. For basic principles of practicing as an expert witness, read the "How to Be an Expert Witness" books recommended in the Resources Section.

ASK FOR REFERRALS

An expert in Houston who has retired from his lifetime career is now a part-time expert witness/consultant, trying to spend time traveling with his wife. He is still besieged with so many calls regarding cases that he turns down enough work to employ one or two other experts full-time. Younger, hungrier experts in his field should be taking him to lunch. Frequently.

When you have finished a case, ask the attorney if he would be so kind as to refer you to other attorneys or give you names of other people he thinks you might assist. This is also the time to request a letter stating that he is pleased with the services you performed.

SEND THANK-YOU NOTES

Be sure to send a thank-you note each time a person, whether attorney, associate, or friend, has referred or recommended you.

After working on a case, send the attorney a thank-you letter in which you include a request for referrals.

NETWORK WITH ATTORNEYS

The most beneficial networking takes place with attorneys themselves. Become acquainted with as many attorneys as possible. Invite them to lunch at your expense. Your $25–$40 investment may be one of the best you will ever make. Experts have told me that lawyers are too busy to go to lunch. Lawyers have told me they never refuse a free lunch!

Dear Robert:

Thank you for telling John Jones about my firm. I appreciate your kind gesture.

You can feel confident that anyone you refer to me will receive our best in professional service and my personal attention.

Sincerely,

A leading litigation attorney and president of her state bar association said she has only been asked to lunch with expert witnesses twice, and she accepted both times. I am reminded of how many dates men miss by assuming the really attractive girls would not go out with them, when those girls are actually sitting at home alone on Saturday night. Never assume. It does not hurt to ask.

⌁ Networking is the ideal opportunity to communicate the value of working with you, without seeming to "sell."

Show Your Communication Skills

Networking gives you the opportunity to demonstrate your communication skills to the attorney. A conversation gives him an impression of how you will be perceived in deposition and in court and whether you listen effectively.

In the February 28, 2000, issue of *Texas Lawyer*, attorney Fred Misko, Jr., said, "After true expertise, the most significant aspect of an expert's qualifications is the ability to communicate convincingly in a litigation environment. This means the ability to deliver and explain opinions persuasively to a jury through expert reports and depositions. If the expert communicates only with other experts within a narrow field and cannot explain complex subjects to the layman, the expert may be worthless in the case."

In Harry Beckwith's book, *The Invisible Touch: The Four Keys to Modern Marketing*, he relates the results of a survey by DecisionQuest, a jury consulting firm, regarding the question: "What makes a juror think that one expert is more expert than the other – and therefore more apt to be believed in the typical battle of experts that often decides the outcome of a trial?"

The result: "Thousands of jurors forced DecisionQuest to accept the surprising but unavoidable conclusion – Credentials do not matter." "What mattered? Who did people think was the more expert expert? The person who most *clearly* communicated her expertise."

The conclusions of Mr. Beckwith, who is an attorney: "Communication is not a skill. It is *the* skill. The best way to demonstrate your expertise is clearly." And, *"You must be clearer. Much, much clearer."*

Convey Your Attitude

In a networking situation the attorney gets to know *who* you are. In directories and other advertising the information listed is *what* you are – your area of specialty, education, experience, and other credentials. In face-to-face encounters you convey your personality and what you will be like to work with in a business relationship. The attorney does not have the expertise or the time to find "the best expert" in the field. He probably would not know when he had found such a person. Instead, he hires the expert with whom he feels the most comfortable.

As you network you must clearly communicate your area of specialty and basic qualifications, but keep in mind that your case review (or even testimony) is not the primary thing you have to offer. It is just the basic feature. Likely there are several, perhaps many, experts in your specialty with your degree(s) or better, and experience of similar value. The major attribute you have to offer is your personal and unique service, created by who you are, what you know, and how you relate to people. As illustrated in "What, Who, and Why," in the chapter on planning, those aspects can be communicated, and should comprise your attitude for networking.

In his first book, *Selling the Invisible: A Field Guide to Modern Marketing*, Harry Beckwith says, "In most professional services, you are not really selling your expertise, because your expertise is assumed, and because your prospective client cannot intelligently evaluate your expertise anyway. Instead, you are selling a *relationship*. And in most cases, that is where you need the most work. If you're selling a service, you're selling a relationship."

GO WHERE THE ATTORNEYS ARE

A competent sales manager tells sales representatives that unless they are on the phone with prospects or clients, they should not be in the office but, instead, "fishing where the fish are." Mix and mingle with attorneys in both professional and social settings.

a) Attend attorney group meetings

Call your local and state bar associations and ask for their policy on non-attorneys attending section meetings. Some will allow you to attend. A few associations even have a membership level for non-legal professionals. You will probably be referred to the chairperson of the section related to your profession. Call and make arrangements to attend a meeting. Attend any functions you can, become acquainted with as many members as possible, and be alert for the opportunity to make a presentation to the group. Always have a supply of business cards with you.

Do not overlook specialty attorney associations, formed according to area of law practiced, e.g., Elder Law or ethnic origin, as well as women attorney and young attorney associations.

If an attorney you meet expresses a desire to see your *c.v.* or other information, promptly respond the next day. Send any appropriate thank-you or other follow-up notes the day after the meeting, while having met you is still fresh in their minds.

b) Attend CLE classes on your subject of expertise

Continuing Legal Education (CLE) classes are a licensing requirement for lawyers. If the subject of a class relates to your area of expertise, you are guaranteed a group of classmates who are your prospects. The Web site of your bar or association will list its CLE calendar. Locate classes for attorneys in your field, and ask whether non-attorneys can attend. For example, non-attorneys are allowed at CLE classes of the Florida Bar Association. Those classes are also announced in *The Florida Bar News*, which welcomes non-attorney subscriptions.

If the bar-sponsored CLE classes are not open to non-attorneys, ask the bar for names of private providers of CLE classes. CLE classes are also provided by universities and even by large law firms.

At classes attended by one expert, some of the attorneys stayed just long enough to sign in, then left to play golf all day, and returned at the very end. So this venue is not guaranteed to be a networking occasion. You might at least have an opportunity to visit at breaks with the attorneys who *teach* the classes, and not all CLE classes are like this.

c) Teach CLE classes for attorneys

Contact the bar association about providing a Continuing Legal Education class for attorneys in your area of specialty, sponsored by the bar. If your material is approved, you could also present it to a law firm or a section of a large law firm.

This is an ideal networking situation. You have the opportunity to let the attorneys get to know you, display your knowledge of your discipline, and demonstrate how effectively you could explain the facts to the jury.

d) Socialize with attorneys at judicial fundraisers

In Texas, attorneys are some of the largest contributors to judicial election campaigns. A Houston CPA who consults on business fraud cases and computes economic damages has been quite successful meeting and visiting with attorneys at judicial fundraisers. He laughingly says that few of his competitors attend since accountants will not attend functions that are not tax deductible!

If you are a heavy voter, i.e., vote in many of the elections for which you are eligible, you probably receive candidate information in the mail and, possibly, invitations to events such as fundraisers. When you receive information or see notices in the newspaper, call the candidate's headquarters and ask to attend his fundraiser. Since campaign workers are constantly seeking new contributors, you will probably be welcomed.

An attorney with whom I consulted cautioned that an expert should be mindful of politics – getting into fundraising events with a friend is better than contributing money and being put on contributor lists. Murphy's Law dictates that you will probably testify before the judge defeated by the candidate you supported.

e) Contribute to and attend attorneys' charity events

Social events are a low-stress networking opportunity. People are more amenable to conversation when they are eating and drinking. There is also an easy camaraderie at work sites. If you see a notice that attorneys or paralegals are, e.g., manning a Christmas tree lot to raise money for charity or painting houses for the homeless, and it states that others are welcome to work with them, show up to help. To find out about these events, call the bar or other attorney association and ask to be put on any mailing list available to non-attorneys, or subscribe to the organization's periodical or newsletter.

f) Meet attorneys speaking at expert witness conferences

In most instances the attorneys who speak at expert witness conferences are litigators. If time is limited, or if originating a conversation would be awkward, simply hand the speaker your card with a gracious, "I know you're rushing for your plane, but I enjoyed your presentation."

g) Become involved with law schools in your area

Meet the professors and explore how you might be of service to them. Find the faculty list on the Web site of the law school nearest you, and locate the professor or professors who teach in your area of law. You can also obtain this information from the school's catalog or on the information board at the school. Call the professor and offer to speak to his class.

Andre Moenssens, the Douglas Stripp Professor of Law at the University of Missouri at Kansas City, said that he brings in actual expert witnesses on a regular basis (and also did so while he was teaching in Chicago and in Richmond, Virginia). He has his students act as lawyers and practice direct and cross-examination of these experts in mock trial or hearing settings. He is grateful for the opportunity to let the students interact with real experts.

How memorable would you be to an attorney if you were the first expert witness he ever met, while he was still in law school?

h) Exhibit at state bar and trial attorney association conventions

The primary benefit of exhibiting comes from meeting attorneys and giving them your promotional material as they stroll through the exhibitor area. Another opportunity for exposure is to advertise in the convention handout information. Sponsoring meals or refreshments at the meetings is not usually cost-effective.

The average exhibitor fee is approximately $1,000 plus expenses. The largest expense is that of purchasing a professional looking booth, which can be $15,000 or more. Experts give exhibiting mixed reviews. Therefore, and also because of the expense, I do not recommend exhibiting for the sole practitioner or small firm unless the exhibitor rate is low and the exhibitor arrangement is informal, e.g., just a table, and therefore less costly.

A guide to legal conventions and trade shows is listed in the Resources section.

NETWORKING SKILLS

a) Practice your statement of profession

A Statement of Profession is a sentence, compound if necessary, stating the services that you or your company provides, and for whom. This is also called a "Defining Statement" or a "Positioning Statement."

Since the first opportunity to make someone aware of and knowledgeable about you is often unexpected and brief, you need to prepare and memorize a short statement of what you do. This statement needs to be concise and yet complete enough to produce referrals from people who hear it. People must be able to understand and remember what you actually *do* as a litigation support consultant. Rehearse your Statement of Profession until reciting it is second nature. A comprehensive yet brief statement of your expertise and services will go a long way in producing referrals.

The maximum length of a Statement of Profession is cocktail party reply or elevator ride length. As you are introduced or introduce yourself, the other person asks, "And what do you do?" If you are in a legal profession setting you respond with a statement of your forensic profession. Common sense and social adeptness dictate a short, succinct reply. The information, nonetheless, needs to be complete enough that the listener will comprehend your area of work well enough to be able to use the information if later confronted with a referring opportunity.

Note: The term "expert witness" is particularly inadequate on its own since a competent expert witness/consultant in most fields actually testifies in few cases.

Examples of Statements of Profession

"I provide litigation support." [In what field?]

"I am an expert witness." [About what?]

"I am an engineer and work with attorneys." [Doing what?]

"I am a structural engineer and help attorneys with their claims" or "I am an engineer and help attorneys with their structural engineering claims, primarily plaintiff." [Good.]

"I am engaged in legal medicine." [In what medical specialty? Furthermore, what does legal-medicine mean to anyone other than an attorney?]

"I am an orthopedic surgeon who specializes in sports medicine and help attorneys with their cases, both plaintiff and defense." [Good.]

If you are a medical expert witness and are speaking to an attorney, you might add to, "I'm a gastroenterologist and review medical records for attorneys," the additional phrase, "and provide testimony if necessary," since some doctors will not testify.

Unique Selling Proposition

Generic sales parlance suggests coining a Unique Selling Proposition. A USP includes, in addition to the above information, the uniqueness and/or benefit of using the speaker's services. In consumer marketing the USP tells the prospect why he should choose to do business with the speaker rather than anyone else or than doing nothing. An example is this Yellow Pages ad for an electrical repair service: "24-Hour Emergency Service, 7 Days. No Job Too Small."

This kind of sales pitch, even if well executed, is inappropriate for an expert in the legal community. Confine the presentation of your services to your Statement of Profession. If a conversation ensues from an introduction, the benefits of using your services can be stated subtly and tastefully later or even conveyed by the questions you ask.

b) Adopt a networking mentality

Be alert to opportunities to meet and talk with attorneys. They can arise unexpectedly. When Stephen Jones, attorney for Timothy McVeigh, spoke at an expert witness conference, his book, *Others Unknown: The Oklahoma City Bombing Case and Conspiracy*, had just been published and the conference holder had copies for sale. I bought three, and Mr. Jones was quite gracious in autographing each one. My objective was to handle three Christmas presents, but what I also got was ten minutes of Mr. Jones' undivided attention as he inscribed the books with a personal note to each recipient. Sad to say, only two experts took advantage of the same opportunity. By the way, Mr. Jones' specialization as a criminal defense attorney would not have nullified the networking opportunity. Attorneys do not associate only with other attorneys in the same specialty.

c) Do not be reticent

Attorneys cannot hire you if they do not know you. Do not be pushy, but introduce yourself and describe what you do. Jack Zimmermann, one of the foremost criminal defense attorneys in Texas, was the lunch speaker at the conference mentioned above. When he finished speaking I handed him my card and simply said, "If you are ever looking for an expert, give me a call; here is my number." He took the card and thanked me. Ten seconds. Low-key. One week later, his daughter and law partner, Terri Jacobs, called me looking for a doctor to review medical records, and I was able to refer a number of doctors to her from my database. One of the experts at that conference, a client of mine, was in front of me, offering Mr. Zimmermann his card. Mr. Zimmermann asked the expert to send him a resume.

COMMUNICATION SKILLS

If you are not accustomed to promoting yourself or your business in personal exchanges, you can err in either of two directions – being too reticent or being obnoxious. Anyone reaching over the tray of strawberries for the chocolate dip at a buffet would become annoyed with a person at his side attempting to "sell" him on his professional acumen. At business gatherings such as CLE classes you can be more overt, as networking is expected. In social settings discretion is required.

The alternate mistake to being overly aggressive is to hesitate to approach possible contacts. Shyness can even appear to be self-centeredness. When you walk into a gathering, either look for a person who looks friendly and open, or adopt a charitable attitude and approach someone who seems to be excluded from the group or a bit "under the weather" and attempt to make him feel more comfortable. The key idea is, "Do not think about yourself; think about the other person."

This applies to the manner in which you converse as well. A friend and former employer of mine, Art Slaton, is considered a great conversationalist. At meetings and parties he rarely volunteers information about himself. Instead, he communicates with relaxed but direct eye contact, and gentle but probing questions, which suggests he genuinely wants to get to know the other person. I doubt that he ever feels that someone is looking for an exit, and the other person always remembers him.

Be Interested, Not Interesting

The key is to be interested, not interesting. Encourage the person to talk about himself, and he will find you interesting! As you engage in normal social banter, ask the attorney:

What type of law do you practice? What do you enjoy about that field? Where did you attend law school? What made you decide to go into law? What has been your most interesting or challenging case?

One topic of conversation that would put you on the interviewing side and also provide valuable data would be to ask the attorney about his experiences with expert witnesses. Has he had good experiences, a particularly interesting one, or a horror story (which everyone loves to relate)?

Get over the misconception that effective selling or promotion lies in "making a business presentation." A former business associate of mine who was making a great deal of money as a mortgage loan officer demonstrated the validity of this principle. When I asked him for the key to his success, he was hard pressed to identify it. I persisted, and he said, "Well, I try not to talk about business when I do business." Although obviously you cannot take that attitude to an extreme, there is a principle to be learned. In a social setting, particularly, make the contact and be clear about what you do, but lighten up. Make your new acquaintance remember you as a friendly, interest*ed* person.

Nametags – a "Little Thing"

At most networking functions and an occasional social event, attendees wear nametags. Rather than just punching another hole in your lapel, make the accessory work for you.

Make certain that your tag shows your name *and field* prominently, so people can relate your identification with your face. If necessary, make your own version of the provided tag or add information to it. Sometimes the name is so small that people cannot read the letters from six inches away.

One woman who was adept at networking had a classy nametag professionally produced, with a very legible rendering of her name, along with her title and company. At events she wears her personal nametag above the furnished event nametag. She even chose a fastener that does not poke a hole in silk blouses.

The next time you attend a function where name badges are furnished, notice where most people are wearing them. The most common location, the center of the chest, is not effective and can be particularly inappropriate for women. No matter where the helpful registrar aims the nametag for you, wear it on your upper right chest, almost up to your shoulder. When people walk up and shake your hand, the badge is near their eye level and they can see your name without losing eye contact. This small point contributes to your graciousness, as people who have forgotten your name can refresh their memory without making a point of looking.

STAY IN TOUCH

Maintaining contact is critical – out of sight is out of the attorney's mind, and out of work. Jim Robinson, attorney and President of JurisPro.com, said, "Practicing regular and persistent follow-up with attorneys has proven to be one of the most important factors in consistent case retentions."

Mr. Robinson also remarked, "One of the best things an expert can do for an attorney is to provide a deposition outline to use in qualifying an expert in his field of discipline. Partners hang onto them, make copies, and give them to younger associates. Have the expert put his contact information on it prominently, and send it out to attorneys."

Remind your client or prospect about you by sending a clipping or a copy of an article that would benefit him, with a brief note, "Thought this might be of interest to you," along with your contact information. A likely topic would be an issue or new development in the field of discipline in which you both work.

C O M M E N T

Networking is defined as trading on established relationships and the exchange of information among individuals, groups, or institutions. Develop your networking skills, and your chances of becoming successful increase exponentially. You will also become a better communicator, meet more people, broaden your horizons, and feel the satisfaction of helping other people, too.

PUBLICITY

Most of it is Free

- Writing
  - Legal Periodicals
  - Trade Journals
  - Books and Papers
  - Consumer (Public) Publications
  - Viewpoints Pages, Letters to Editors, Book Reviews, National Advice Columns
- Speaking
  - Trade or Professional Meetings
  - Expert Witness Conferences
  - Attorney CLE Classes
  - Public (Community) Events
- Electronic Media
  - Radio
  - TV
  - Electronic Publicity Tips
- Professional Announcements and News Releases
  - Professional Announcements
    - Themes for Professional Announcements
    - How to Produce a Professional Announcement
  - News Releases
    - How to Produce a News Release
- Media Kit
- Public Relations Firms and Media Consultants

∽ **When your expertise is publicized** in articles and books or on radio or television, it does not look like advertising, it does not feel like advertising, but, delightfully, it works like advertising. Publicity is, in fact, the best promotional avenue after networking. Even better – it is usually inexpensive or even free.

WRITING
a) Legal Periodicals

Many legal newspapers, magazines, and journals will accept articles from non-attorneys on a subject that will benefit their readers. Appearing in publications as a writer confers credibility and authority upon the author.

By submitting your article for a publication section that focuses on a particular area of law, you can specifically target your potential clients. Call the publishing office and request a calendar of special sections to be published on particular topics so you can volunteer to write a pertinent article.

Whether writing for the main body of a periodical or a special section, find the name of the editor in the publication's masthead (staff list), or call to obtain the information. Contact the editor and offer an article of interest to his readers.

Gaining acceptance of your article is a separate transaction from advertising in the same publication. An ethical publication separates journalism from advertising. Your article should be accepted or rejected on its own merit, and not be influenced by the fact that you might be an advertiser.

b) Trade Journals

Writing for your industry accomplishes several things. Being published engenders instant respect from your peers, who know how challenging it is to write anything of substance. Also, whether or not litigation consulting is the focus of your article, you can communicate to your peers directly or indirectly that you do forensic work, and thereby develop referral sources. If an attorney consults trade journals to find experts, you will stand out.

A caution from the publishing world: Show respect for the editor. On occasion people have not gotten the cooperation they wanted from their industry publications because of failing to treat the publishing staff with the professional respect they might have shown *The Wall Street Journal* staff, for example. Realize that the editor at the trade publication may have been hired away from *TWSJ*.

c) Books and Papers

Writing books and papers, especially those for peer review, elevates your professional status and lends credibility to your resume. Your profession may even require that you have peer-reviewed, published works. Another reason for writing is that attorneys search the Internet for publications related to the subjects of their cases in order to find related, qualified expert witnesses. Being a published author can create additional publicity in the form of media interviews, book signings, and book reviews. While writing requires a tremendous effort, the benefits of being published definitely make the effort worthwhile.

d) Consumer (Public) Publications

Reporters and editors seek out experts to comment on current news items. They maintain a large card file of people who can provide a "sound bite" spontaneously for print or air. To meet journalists, call your local newspaper and radio and television stations and ask whether they have, e.g., a medical editor. Call and introduce yourself and offer to take him to lunch to get acquainted and determine whether you could ever be of service. Sometimes this works, sometimes not. Even one successful contact could provide valuable public exposure and enhance your credibility as an expert in your field.

e) Viewpoints Pages, Letters to Editors, Book Reviews, National Advice Columns

Remember that these reach the general consumer rather than targeting the legal community, and therefore do not merit as much of your effort as do legal publications. They are, however, free forums and, in many cases, widely read. Remember to identify yourself and list your contact information on any writing you submit for publication.

C A U T I O N

Do not submit your writing to a publication you have not read. Look over the entire publication, not just your portion of interest. Get a sense of the publication and its readers.

SPEAKING

a) Trade or Professional Meetings

Presenting yourself and your ideas before a professional group can raise your professional stature in the same way as writing. If your topic is not related to litigation, include in your remarks that you engage in litigation support as a part of your profession. You never know who in your audience can become a prospective client or a referral source.

b) Expert Witness Conferences

Offer to speak at conferences of experts on a topic of general interest to all experts or on a topic in your field. The better known and respected you become by your peers, the more chances you have of being referred by a person you might not have even met personally.

c) Attorney CLE Classes

Ask attorneys what information from experts would help them with their cases, and prepare a presentation. Ask your local and state bar associations for their policy on non-attorney speakers for Continuing Legal Education and approval procedures for your presentation. For their speaking policy, you may be referred to the chairperson of your industry related attorney section.

Alternately, if you obtain permission to speak to a group of attorneys at a firm that specializes in your area of expertise, they may apply for the CLE accreditation. Even so, you will want to already be familiar with the CLE requirement forms so that your presentation will be in the proper format to facilitate accreditation.

If you are not furnished a list of attendees, create a reason to collect their business cards, e.g., to send a copy of your presentation or an article you mention in your presentation.

d) Public (Community) Events

Legal affairs are one of the so-called "sexy subjects." Most people find the legal world fascinating. Clubs, lodges, and associations are continually recruiting speakers. Volunteer to speak, and ask if they would like to hear about your experience with lawyers and the courts (the parts you can share).

If you happen to speak on a non-legal topic, mention that part or all of your work is litigation-related. Thoroughly identify yourself and list your contact information on your handouts at a speaking event. Have plenty of your business cards on hand as well.

When presenting at community events, speak in layman's language and be entertaining. Remember that no one is as interested in your subject as you are. And practice. Appearing effortless takes a lot of effort!

ELECTRONIC MEDIA

Most expert consultants will not pursue radio or television publicity. The process is easier, however, than you might think. Start with your local program director or station manager, who can help you in contacting people at the national level.

a) Radio

You have a good chance of being invited to speak on local talk shows if you simply contact them. As various issues are addressed in public forums, the FCC requires airtime responses to those issues. Since someone's comments will be aired, make the stations aware of your expertise so you will come to mind when they need a statement from a person in your discipline.

b) TV

To use television as a publicity avenue, start with a Sunday morning public affairs interview at the local cable television stations. Their producers seek out interesting guests, and legal issues appeal to most of the general public. If you are qualified to comment on a current news topic, offer to present your viewpoint.

Electronic Publicity Tips

You can apply to radio and television producers to appear on their shows. Send a single-page letter of three paragraphs, without hype, stating why you should be interviewed. You can also include a list of ten or fifteen sample questions that they might wish to ask you in an interview. You can give both the questions and the answers. This list can be two pages long.

Familiarizing yourself with titles of staff members at radio or TV stations will help you. The information is available at the public library. Since the individual names change, you have to call to determine the current ones.

To prepare for public appearances, consult books on interviewing appearance, style and mannerisms, what to expect, and how to control the interview. Consider investing in media coaching. What those trainers will pound into you on brevity will help you in the courtroom as well.

Listen to or watch, preferably several times, any show to which you might apply. Acquaint yourself with the format and the personality of the show before you submit an application.

PROFESSIONAL ANNOUNCEMENTS AND NEWS RELEASES
a) Professional Announcements

A professional announcement is a dignified method used regularly by attorneys for their own promotion. The advertising industry calls them "tombstones." They are styled like graduation announcements and wedding invitations, usually written in third person ("… is pleased to announce …"). Professional announcements should be formal, rather than sounding like a sales pitch. The purpose is to remind prospective clients of your area of expertise and your availability. Professional announcements are image advertising; they are not designed necessarily to solicit an immediate response. In addition to being printed in periodicals, they can be mailed to your database of clients, prospects, and referral sources.

Changes in your status, events in your professional life, and holiday greetings provide opportunities for professional announcements. I have even seen an announcement saying, basically, "We Sure Told 'em Litigation Associates P.C. is proud to announce their involvement with the law firm of We Got 'em the Money L.L.P. in the successful litigation of Wrongee versus Wrong-er, in which a settlement of $10 million was obtained."

Themes for Professional Announcements

• Opened a practice
• Added an associate
• Promoted an associate
• Congratulated an associate upon a lifetime of achievement at retirement

- Accepted a new partner
- Acquired new shareholder(s)
- Opened an office
- Added a new division, a new lab, or other new facilities
- Moved the office
- Changed a phone or fax number or email address
- Appointed to a teaching position
- Appointed to a government advisory committee
- Published a paper in a professional journal
- Published a book
- Discovered a new method of solving a business problem, made a medical discovery, or perfected a technique
- Received an award for excellence in a professional endeavor
- Completed a training program
- Qualified for a certification
- Received a grant to pursue research
- Earned an additional degree
- Formed an organization
- Appointed or elected to a position in an organization
- Created or revised a Web site
- Consulted in a case resulting in a substantial verdict (Request prior clearance from the law firm.)
- Commemorated a milestone year in your specialty or in litigation support, or in a geographical area
- Performed public service (an effective theme)
- Recognized by a law firm with which you are associated
- The latest development taking place in your professional field, especially as it affects lawyers (Be sure to keep commercialism to a minimum.)
- Celebration of holidays

The components of a professional announcement are:
- The event
- Who you are
- A carefully worded statement of your area of expertise and/or services
- Contact information

CHOOSE AN EVENT TO ANNOUNCE. You can also explain how the event, e.g., a move to larger quarters with more convenient client parking, will help you better serve your clients, as long as you do not get schmaltzy.

CLEARLY IDENTIFY YOUR FIRM. If the individual or firm name or logo does not include field of expertise, put that information in the text. For example, if an accounting firm is named Adams & Black, P.C., rather than Adams & Black, CPA's, P.C., state the field of Forensic Accounting.

BRIEFLY DESCRIBE YOUR SERVICES. Following the above example, list sub-specialties of Economic Damages, Fraud Investigation, and Business Valuation. Remember that the topic of the announcement is simply an excuse to remind clients, prospects, and referral sources about your services.

FOR CONTACT INFORMATION include, at a minimum, your phone number, Web site address if you have one, and mailing address if there is enough space.

For a formal look, select a high-grade paper or cardstock to tuck inside an envelope, like this announcement from Nelson Architectural Engineers. Hand-address the envelopes and use individual postage stamps. Hire a student to do both of these tasks. (Buy the stamps yourself so you do not end up with a heart or butterfly design.)

Nelson Architectural Engineers, Inc.
*is pleased to announce we have expanded our Forensic Services
to include Indoor Air Quality (IAQ) Testing and Consulting.*

Please contact us for questions regarding:

• Air Sampling	• Aspergillus & Stachybotrys
• Contamination	• Sick Building Syndrome
• Remediation	• Mold/Fungus (Mycology)

Offices in Dallas and Houston

3303 Lee Parkway, Suite 440 Dallas, Texas 75219-5116 *tel* 214-528-8765 *fax* 214-528-3244
toll free 1-877-850-8765 *e-mail* archengr@airmail.net www.architecturalengineers.com

Telaclaim™ - Online request for engineering services

You can have announcements commercially printed and cut as postcards at a lower cost, which might be a key factor as your mailing list becomes large. The card from Electrical Expert, Inc. was printed on white cardstock and mailed without an envelope. To help reduce expenses you can print address labels with your computer. The lower cost of postcard mailings enables you to send announcements more frequently. A consistent postcard mailing program is covered in the chapter on direct mail.

Professional announcements should be mailed to clients, prospects, associates, friends, family, and media – i.e., anyone who can provide business to you directly or indirectly.

Erik Nelson, PH.D., of Nelson Architectural Engineers, Inc. in Dallas, mails 1,000-5,000 announcements (depending upon the

Electrical Expert, Inc.

announces that

B. Michael Aucoin, D.Engr., P.E.

has completed the course

Investigating and Litigating Utility Contact Accidents

Myrtle Beach, South Carolina
May, 2001

For more information, contact:

B. Michael Aucoin, D.Engr., P.E.

Electrical Expert, Inc.

Electrical Engineering Litigation Support

PO Box 10597
College Station, Texas 77842

Phone: 979-695-9043
E-mail: maucoin@elec-exp.com
www.elec-exp.com

subject matter and appropriate target list), at least four times a year. He reports receiving calls from people he has not heard from in a long time, resulting in at least one or two cases from each mailing. This expenditure is quite cost-effective.

In addition to printing and mailing professional announcements, you can have them published in legal newspapers, magazines, and journals as advertising.

A new, low-cost venue for announcements is e-mail. Educate yourself on Internet rules for sending unsolicited e-mail and also procedures to simply avoid annoying people with your e-mail traffic.

b) News Releases

News releases were called press releases prior to electronic media. While a news release is related to a professional announcement, it must have news value to the readers of the publication or audience of the medium. Common sense should dictate which of the above list of themes is newsworthy, but this varies with the type and size of the medium. Publications for a small group or in a small geographic region will print items not considered newsworthy in a larger venue. Study the medium to determine what will be published or aired.

How to Produce a News Release

As a news release is printed at no cost to you, control is in the hands of the publication. You must follow the accepted, strict format of a news release, or risk rejection. Furthermore, if the content reads as too promotional, the news release will not be published.

Inquire whether the publication prefers a news release on paper or on disk.

Use letter-size paper, not legal.

NEWS RELEASE: *For Immediate Release*

Contact: Dr. Sarkar, President
Sarkar & Associates, Inc.
Phone: 713-686-0638
Fax: 713-263-0550

HOUSTON CONSULTANT RECEIVES INTERNATIONAL AWARD

Dr. Shondeep L. Sarkar, PE, a Houston-based consultant on construction materials failure and deterioration, and a researcher at the Texas Transportation Institute, Texas A&M University, has just received the prestigious American Concrete Institute - CANMET award. The award presentation was held at the Fifth ACI-CANMET International Conference, held in Barcelona, Spain. Dr. Sarkar received the award for his outstanding and sustained contribution in the field of concrete durability for the past 25 years.

Dr. Sarkar, President of Sarkar & Associates, Inc., has an extensive international background in consulting, research and teaching in England, Nigeria, Canada and the United States. A dedicated researcher and writer, Dr. Sarkar has published more than 150 articles in peer-reviewed journals and international conference proceedings. In addition, he is the editor of the book entitled **Mineral Admixtures in Cement and Concrete** and serves on the editorial board of **World Cement**, an international scientific journal.

- more -

Houston Consultant Receives International Award, pg. 2

Dr. Sarkar's knowledge, know-how and technology in construction materials science is regularly utilized nationally and internationally by civil engineering firms, insurance companies, cement and concrete producers and law firms and by government agencies in the Houston area.

Sarkar & Associates, Inc. offers a range of services that includes testing analysis and troubleshooting for new and existing structures, forensic investigations, R & D in product development related to cement, concrete, and allied construction materials, and expertise in technology transfer.

***

Type on one side only, to allow for cutting and pasting. Do not exceed two pages.

For years the rules have forbade using letterhead stationery, but I now see news releases on stationery.

Leave at least an inch at the bottom of the page, and more if you are between paragraphs. If the document is two pages, type "- more -" at the bottom of the first page, centered.

Double-space the body, which should be upper and lower case. Use single spacing to separate certain content, such as a quotation from a medical journal, from the main text.

Compose short paragraphs of three short sentences, preferably less than forty words per paragraph.

Put the Release Date at top left, five spaces below either the letterhead or the upper edge of the paper. Either use all caps or capitalize the first letter of each of the words. For Immediate Release is better, as editors often ignore the dates anyway.

Three spaces below, put Contact name and phone and fax numbers, or For Further Information Contact.

The Headline, centered, goes three spaces below the contact information and three spaces above the lead paragraph. Using all caps is not necessary but make the headline stand out from the rest of the copy in one way or another – italics, different typeface, or boldface. The headline does not have to be a complete sentence. It can also be a question or a quotation and should interest the reader and encourage further reading. Study newspapers for examples.

In contrast to other types of writing, the significance of a release is expressed in an inverted pyramid. Who, what, where, when, and why go in the first or the first and second paragraphs and should summarize your entire message. List facts in descending order of importance. The lead paragraph is more important than the body paragraph, which is more important than a third paragraph, which is not always necessary, and there is a concluding paragraph.

The conclusion is a concise summary of the primary angle, or additional information that is relevant but not critical enough to have been included earlier. Conclusions differ from all other paragraphs because of a sense of finality.

If you include biographical information on a release, it should be a brief description of credentials, a summary of one's life *as it applies to the primary angle of the release*. Do not state "*our* company" or "I", except in a quote. Write "*the* company" instead.

Center three asterisks at the end to signify the end of the news release.

Do not staple the pages.

The news release can be mailed, faxed or e-mailed, and preferably is addressed to a person's name, not just a position title.

You can attach a photograph, but there is no guarantee it will be used.

MEDIA KIT

A media kit, formerly called a press kit, contains items such as a news release, background information, suggested questions, news clippings, and photographs, primarily for the purpose of eliciting interview requests. A media kit is beyond the scope of most expert consultants' marketing and needed by very few. If you choose to create one, I recommend hiring a public relations service to design and produce the kit.

PUBLIC RELATIONS FIRMS AND MEDIA CONSULTANTS

You can also employ a public relations firm to seek publicity opportunities and present you in a favorable light. You, however, are already familiar with the associations, conventions, conferences, and journals of your trade or profession. Therefore, it would be more cost-effective to get help only with writing or speech composition, or simply arrange for coaching before dealing with live media. Most expert consultants can conduct adequate publicity activities for their practice on their own and engage help on an as-needed basis only.

CAUTION

All of your writing and speaking is discoverable and can be cussed and discussed with you in deposition and in court. Be careful. Be consistent. Investigate, verify, and cross-examine your facts. Proofread, proofread, and proofread again.

DIRECT MAIL

What to Send and to Whom

When you think of direct mail you probably envision an unsolicited, introductory letter to a large number of prospects. Certainly that marketing project falls under the heading of direct mail, but unsolicited mail to random names is not the most productive use of direct mail. The direct mail marketing that is most essential for your business is sending communication pieces frequently and consistently to the same people. For an expert consultant those people are clients, prospects, and potential referral sources, including associates, former co-workers, professional vendors, family, and friends.

First, in our culture of information overload, the number of communications needed for a person to recall what he has seen has probably expanded beyond the traditional three. Busy people have to be reminded on a regular basis in order for you to appear on the radar screen of their consciousness. Second, you have the opportunity to communicate noteworthy events that enhance your professional image and increase perception of your value. Third, people who receive mail from you regularly recognize that they matter to you.

The best use of regular mailings is for sending professional announcements to remind prospects and referral sources of you and your services and enhance your image. A newsletter has similar objectives. The differences: 1) Professional announcements are easier and less costly to produce and mail, and likely to be read by the recipient sooner than a newsletter, and 2) Newsletters require a great deal of effort to produce and are more costly, which makes its own statement about your professional stature. Also, newsletters have a lot of space in which to present articles, news, and comments, i.e., a forum in which to present you and your services in a favorable light.

In contrast to regular mailings, such as professional announcements, the purpose of mailing a letter and an expert's credentials, unsolicited, is to generate requests for further information for current or future cases or, at the least, to result in the recipient filing the information for future use. This is called an introductory or solicitation mailing.

When people cite the "return rate" on direct mail, they are most likely thinking of a one-time solicitation mailing. The actual success rate of sending a quarterly professional announcement or newsletter is more difficult to track precisely. Nonetheless, in the long run, the results from consistent mailings to your own list, even if only twice a year, will become clear to you.

INTRODUCTORY MAILINGS

There is a wide variance in viewpoints as to the effectiveness of promotion by direct mail. With a return, frequently, of only 1–2%, you might feel that such a response rate does not justify the work and expense of preparing and mailing information. A few people experience a much higher return, but they are in the minority. If, however, you mail 1,000 packages at a cost of $1 each and receive ten calls, two or three of which become cases, this is cost-effective.

One factor in your response ratio with introductory mailings is your selection of target prospects. For example, if you work primarily for litigators, yet send letters to an entire bar list, almost half of your mailing is wasted. Even better targeting would be to select only attorneys who specialize in your area of expertise. Furthermore, there is no point in sending a letter to a law firm without addressing it to a specific person's name; such a letter almost certainly goes in the trash unread.

An unsolicited information package sent to an attorney should consist of a brief cover letter, a business card, and an abbreviated *curriculum vitae* called a biographical sketch for an individual, or a simple brochure for a firm. Limiting the contents to these items should keep the cost of preparing and sending the mailing under a dollar. More extensive information such as a multi-page *c.v.* or a large brochure or portfolio should be sent only to prospective clients who request additional information.

Direct mail marketing tips suggest coding your mail pieces in order to track results from specific mailings. This procedure is only practical when respondents return an item such as an order form or a return envelope or a postcard, so is usually not applicable to experts' mailings. You will generally be aware of the results from an introductory mailing. Typically, the response is a phone call from the attorney or his paralegal.

Mailing Lists

Although in this Information Age buying or renting mailing lists is not always necessary, obtaining lists of attorneys on disk or labels does make large mailing projects easy. Be as specific as possible when choosing the categories of attorneys who are your most likely prospects. Also, because 15–25% of the population moves each year, verify that the list is cleaned regularly. This is part of the service for which you are paying.

Start first by asking for list availability at the state bar membership department and also the plaintiff and defense organizations in your state. The state bar usually offers lists sorted not only geographically but also by area of specialty.

Most lists available for rent specify a one-time use with no retention. The association membership secretary or list broker will inform you of the restrictions when you inquire. If the list is for one-time use only, follow the rules – this is a legal issue. If you can purchase the list to be used more than once, add the names into your database and note where you obtained them. This is one way to expand your own database. Use the return mail to further clean the list.

PROFESSIONAL ANNOUNCEMENTS

A large number of acceptable reasons for sending an announcement are listed in the publicity chapter. Although certain topics, such as changes in the firm's working hours or improved parking facilities, might be too informal for a professional announcement that you publish in a periodical, they might be fine for a direct mailing.

Be smart about the topic and the timing of your mailing. Besides noting changes in your life and business, you might think you should pick standard holidays for mailing topics. Yet, most individuals to whom you send Christmas/Hanukkah/Ramadan cards never see them; a secretary opens the cards and tapes them to a door. If you want to send a holiday card, send a New Year's card or, better yet, a Thanksgiving card. These will be noticed and probably passed on to the attorney or insurance executive.

Postcard Announcement

We've engineered and built a website!

www.centerlineconsulting.biz

30 years "Dirty Hands" Road Construction and Materials Engineering Experience

Centerline Consulting
The Paving Experts

Providing Consulting, Dispute Resolution and Expert Witness Services.

850-609-3106

The ideal schedule is a minimum of four mailings a year, perhaps even six. I call these mailings "Howdy Cards." They are simply reminders of you and your services. In our overly busy culture, consistent reminders are a necessity.

You can send nice quality cards or folded pieces in envelopes. On certain occasions, the added touch of using an envelope is appropriate. For regular, consistent mailings, however, I recommend postcards, either large or small, for two reasons: 1) when the person goes through his mail he cannot help but see at a glance the information on the card, whereas the envelope may go into a stack for later reading, and 2) the production cost and postage for a postcard is much less than for an envelope and enclosure.

Postcards can be professionally printed and can represent you and your services quite acceptably. Hand-addressing postcards is probably a waste of extra time and effort, as doing so does not produce the same effect as hand-addressing an envelope. Printing large numbers of address labels from mailing lists or your database for postcards is not only simple and inexpensive, but also acceptable.

NEWSLETTERS

Just as with a professional announcement, the cost-effectiveness of newsletters cannot be measured in the same way as an introductory solicitation mailing. A return on your investment of time and money may not show immediately, and perhaps never in a way you can precisely attribute to the newsletter. A newsletter is, instead, a powerful tool to create credibility, fashion a professional image, and build loyalty. It can also serve as a lead generator, and will do so over time.

The downside of producing a newsletter is the work involved in composing it. The administrative tasks – actually putting the pieces together and getting it printed, labeled, and mailed – are the easy part. Articles and other items must be written or obtained, and many people decide that the deadline pressure is too great. Before committing to a specific newsletter schedule, be sure that you have adequate time and assistance.

Due to the effort required and also the cost of preparation and mailing, I usually do not recommend that sole practitioners use this marketing avenue.

Newsletter Content

In determining what to put into a newsletter ask yourself how you can help the reader. Promote yourself and your services in an oblique way, not directly, or the reader will be turned off. A newsletter should have regular features, that is, certain items that are consistent from issue to issue, preferably in the same location on the page. Regular segments might include a message from you or another person in your industry on trends or forecasts, information on current or proposed legislation, a technical news report on new technology or equipment in the industry, a personal or company profile, e.g., client of the month, an industry calendar of upcoming events, an interview, or a column of questions and answers.

Photos, graphics, and cartoons are invitations to read. Another tip for reader attention: A newsletter is not the place for long articles. Short articles invite the reader to a quick read; long articles qualify for a place in one's reading stack for later.

Eliciting feedback is a principal benefit of a newsletter. Feedback involves the reader, confirms readership, builds your database, and develops relationships. Examples of feedback requests are offers of a full reprint of a synopsized article, a copy of your *c.v.*, a sample case, or the addition of the reader's associate to the newsletter mailing list. Make it easy for the reader to call, write, fax, or e-mail the feedback. Create the feedback request to capture as much information as possible from the feedback, to update and enhance your database.

The Expert Witness Marketing Book

Newsletter Mailing List

Purchased mailing lists are not appropriate for newsletters. Newsletters are collegial, so build and refine your own list of clients, targeted prospective clients, associates, and other referral sources.

Generic Newsletters

Be cautious about using a generic industry newsletter, which is purchased ready-made and your firm's information simply inserted as though you had created the newsletter. The publisher should certify that he will not sell to another firm of the same type within a geographic area. Even so, using these newsletters is risky in this age of invisible borders. (I received from two different accounting firms newsletters that were identical except for the senders.) I suspect that wrongful portrayal of authorship might even be used to destroy credibility in cross-examination.

Newsletter Construction

Save money by using standard sized paper. Standard printer stock, $8 \frac{1}{2} \times 11$ inches, can be printed front and back, or stock 17 inches wide $\times$ 11 inches deep can be folded to a size of $8 \frac{1}{2} \times 11$ inches.

The format should remain consistent in margins and column widths from issue to issue.

Your newsletter is not required reading, so make it inviting. Break the text into digestible pieces. If you are listing several points, number them or bullet-point them. Subtitles help break up long passages. Underline them or select bold type.

It should go without saying that once you have decided on type font and size and color they should remain the same. The exception: Color is better than black-and-white, but if you cannot afford color in the beginning, do not hesitate to send black-and-white if you have worthwhile messages to communicate. Switch to color when your budget supports the upgrade.

POSTAL INFORMATION

If you mail your own pieces rather than using a mailing house you will need to learn about postage rates and terminology. For instance, if you mail at bulk rate, which is considerably cheaper than first class, there are requirements as to how the mail is sorted by zip code and the minimum numbers of pieces in each zip code. (Do not mail professional announcements that are enclosed in an envelope at less than first class.) Mailing at bulk rate means that the undeliverable mail is thrown away, and mail addressed to a person who has moved will not be forwarded.

If you pay first class rates, the mail will be forwarded. The mail to addresses for which forwarding information has expired, along with mail to inaccurate or incomplete addresses, will be returned to you. Research the information and update your database.

It is imperative that you or an assistant understands the Special Address Services, also called Ancillary Service Endorsements, of the U.S. Post Office, particularly for bulk rate mailings. The titles sound similar, but they indicate different services and cost different rates. They are Address Service Requested, Return Service Requested, Forward Service Requested, and Change Service Requested. You can use an endorsement to change how the Post Office treats your first class mail, and it is essential that you use one for bulk mailing. The endorsement dictates whether pieces are returned to you or forwarded, and whether a corrected address is returned to you. Using an endorsement requires that you decide whether to, e.g., a) pay the cheaper bulk mail rate plus the fee for having undeliverables returned for a certain fee, or b) pay the first class rate and have the undeliverables returned at no additional cost and the others forwarded, but without learning the new address. Another option is to have the pieces forwarded

The Expert Witness Marketing Book

but receive a card from the Post Office with the new forwarding address. These decisions are not just for cost budgeting, but also for database management purposes.

C A U T I O N

Since postal regulations change frequently, check for the latest information at www.usps.com in a section called Business Mail 101.

MAILING SERVICES

I have found the cost of using a mailing house, also called a letter shop, to be a good value. Not only are their services reasonably priced, but they also stay up-to-date on postal regulations so that you do not have to take the time to do so. In addition, you can use their bulk mail permit number instead of acquiring your own.

There are companies that not only label and mail your postcard promotions, but also can help you design them. Some companies have a minimum order. Others might not, but could cost considerably more, so shop for price as well as quality.

DIRECT MAIL BY E-MAIL

Promotional mailings as well as newsletters can now be sent by e-mail. The advantage is obvious – low, low cost. Another advantage is that e-mail is intrusive, similar to faxes. The recipient nearly always notices that he has received an e-mail, whereas he may not see all of his mail if someone else opens it.

The disadvantages are that e-mail is not yet as universal as postal mail, the piece is not tangible, and its shelf life is usually shorter. In addition, the issue of spamming poses a disadvantage to e-mail compared to bulk postal mail. (Spamming is slang for Unsolicited Commercial E-Mail, UCE, which is sending unsolicited e-mails to large groups of people who do not know you). Your Internet Service Provider can limit your out-going e-mail traffic or even disconnect your service for spamming or appearing to spam. Obtaining mailing addresses is also easier than finding e-mail addresses in a niche (not general consumer) market.

COMMENT

The primary objective of introductory mailings to a rented list of names is to generate a few responses. The purpose of regular, consistent mailings to a list of your own is to build a base of business and a referral network, from which you might ultimately draw almost all of your business. This is the golden goose.

REFERRAL SERVICES

How They Work

CHAPTER TEN GUIDE

- Overview
- Application Questions
- Operating Methods
- Charges and Payments
- References
- Medical Referral Agency
- Internet-Only Referral Services
- National Databases
  - Association of Trial Lawyers of America
  - Defense Research Institute

ᴗᴏ Registering with a referral service is a valid marketing avenue for the expert just starting his litigation practice. This is also a good choice for an experienced expert who has a narrow, or esoteric, field. An attorney is more likely to use a referral service for an unusual specialty than he is for a more common one. In addition, a referral service is a marketing and administrative option for a physician wishing to do Independent Medical Evaluations.

OVERVIEW

Referral services are also called brokers, referral agencies, or consulting agencies.

Referral services charge the attorney, the expert, or both. (Professional membership organizations of experts, such as accountants and engineers, usually refer attorneys to their members free of charge.)

Commercial referral services promote their service to attorneys, who contact them when they need experts. The service then calls an expert who is registered with them or, if they do not have that particular kind of expert, attempts to locate one.

When a law firm engages you through certain referral services, any future work you do for that law firm may be under contract with the referral service for a specified period. This is a matter for consideration due to the high value of repeat and referral work. Nonetheless, registering with a referral service is a way to get work, usually at no cost to you.

The referral service, or agency, should have a large number of experts registered. Find out how many. If the agency is a sham, having few or no experts registered, and only searches for an expert when an attorney calls, you do not want your name and resume to be the decoy. Ask how the agency's services are promoted to attorneys. Many of the effective ones advertise extensively in legal publications. If attorneys do not know about the agency, registering with that agency will not be beneficial to you.

APPLICATION QUESTIONS

You will have to give a referral service the information they need to market your services. This information includes, e.g., how many cases in which you have been involved, numbers of depositions and court testimony, and percentage of plaintiff and defense cases. Another question is what percentage of your income comes from litigation support. A doctor will be asked whether he has been sued, and the outcome of the lawsuits. Do not be offended at their questions, as they will need the data, but you can see why registering only with reputable services is critical.

OPERATING METHODS

The methods of operation vary. They are usually one or a hybrid of the following:

- The service simply gives the attorney one or more names and addresses and/or phone numbers of people possessing the credentials he is seeking.
- The service pre-screens the experts' credentials and actually recommends a particular expert.
- The service acts as a general contractor. For instance, the attorney sends medical records to the agency, which then sends them to a doctor. The agency forwards the completed report to the attorney, sometimes with no communication having taken place between the attorney and the expert.
- The service, particularly a medical agency, reviews the case first, determining which specialty the attorney needs, and then forwards the records to the expert.

Some of the agencies listed in the Referral section of the Resources section feel strongly about the differences in method of operation, so much so that they prefer to be called consulting services. I find this attitude most prevalent in the medical field.

CHARGES AND PAYMENTS

There are two fee issues. One is the fee for the referral process, and the other is the fee for the expert's services.

The attorney or the insurance company usually pays the referral fee. Less common is charging the expert, and even less common is charging both the attorney or insurance company and the expert.

In regard to the expert's services, if the agency charges the attorney a flat fee (finder's fee) for the referral, you will probably make your own arrangements with the attorney for your services and will also be responsible for collecting payment. Alternately, the agency may add an amount or a percentage to your services rate, in which case they will likely handle the billing and collecting of the entire fee from the attorney. In this circumstance you would be paid by the referral agency for your services. Under this arrangement there would probably be no separate referral fee.

TASA is the best-known expert witness referral service, advertising consistently in the majority of the legal publications across the country. They typically add $80–$90 per hour to the hourly fee of experts, unless the expert's normal hourly rate is less than $90, in which case TASA doubles that fee.

Read the contract carefully. A critical issue is how the billing is handled. Who actually does the billing? More importantly, who *collects* the fee from the attorney? How are you paid? The other key point to analyze is how long you will be obligated to the service, if at all, for additional cases from law firms they broker for you.

Do not be naive; recognize that you are working in the legal arena. Analyze the potential for a scenario such as this: the law firm fails to pay you, but, because of the contract wording, you are still obligated to pay the referral service. Address such issues thoroughly before signing a contract.

Be aware that being on contract with a referral service may very well be brought up at trial. Like other cross-examination points, this issue is neither positive nor negative at face value. You should respond to questions non-defensively and with poise. Just bear in mind that the question can come up. A reasonable response is that "listing one's business services with a referral agency is an expected part of doing business."

REFERENCES

There are good expert witness referral services, and some not so good. A reputable one will give you the names and numbers of a few experts they have served. Do not bluff by just asking for references – call and talk to them. One reference is not sufficient; obtain at least three. Some people are ineffective at turning information requests into business and blame the marketing medium. On the other hand, talking to only one reference with a good report could mean simply that you talked to the referral service operator's loyal nephew.

MEDICAL REFERRAL AGENCY

For doctors, working through a medical referral agency can be a sensible option. If a doctor is not familiar with the ins and outs of the legal process, he may dispense free information or for less than he could have charged. In addition, his office staff members might not be trained in the litigation consulting aspect of his business, e.g., not know how to bill and collect appropriately. In this case, he may be better off paying an agency an administrative fee or accepting a discounted rate for his services in return for their handling the financial matters. By arranging for the agency to bill and collect from the attorney or insurance company and then pay him, he could end up making more money, as well as saving himself a headache.

INTERNET-ONLY REFERRAL SERVICES

Internet-only referral services are listed in the Resources section under Referral Services. The expert listings on their Web sites are not available to the attorney or any other searcher free of charge, as they are in most directories on the Internet. This makes them referral services, not directories. Be especially demanding as to how Internet-only referral services advertise to attorneys. You cannot depend on the attorney finding the site with just search engines.

JurisSolutions.com uses an interesting combination system of listing experts openly on the site, as a directory, and also operating a referral service offering verified experts, particularly medical experts, for a fee.

NATIONAL DATABASES

The ATLA and DRI expert witness databases are not standard referral services. They are open only to their members and are not involved in the case beyond making information about the expert witness available to the attorney.

Association of Trial Lawyers of America

The ATLA Exchange Expert Witness Directory provides ATLA member attorneys with the names of experts on specific products, techniques, injuries, and issues. Attorneys might have already submitted information about you, but by entering yourself, you can correct or update the data. To be listed in the database you can pay a fee, receive a discount on the rate as a consequence of also advertising in *TRIAL* magazine, or ask an ATLA attorney for whom you have consulted to send ATLA a letter about you.

Defense Research Institute

The DRI Expert Witness Database is available only to members, who pay a nominal fee to access the database. There is no charge for the expert witness to list his services.

⁓ There are valid reasons for some experts to use a referral service. As with all sources of business, choose carefully, ask a lot of questions, particularly about financial arrangements, and check references.

ADVERTISING

Whether, Where, and How

CHAPTER ELEVEN GUIDE

- How Much to Spend on Advertising
- Types of Advertising
  - Display Advertising
    - Designing a Display Ad
    - Professional Announcement
  - Classified Advertising
    - Classified Advertising – A Long-Term Run
- Proofreading Your Ad
- Purchasing Advertising
- Specialty Advertising

To experts who say, "I do not need to advertise; I have all the business I need," I quote Confucius, "Dig the well before you thirst." In fact, one of the most perilous times in a business is when the business seems to have finally taken off, with a sufficient amount of work to be solvent and profitable. Murphy's Law being immutable, after the current business engagements are handled, the business may dry up without warning and, seemingly, with no explanation.

In my many years of working with expert witnesses, even after pointing to tort reform or the threat thereof, recession economies, and other vagaries, sometimes there seems to be no reasonable explanation for calls from attorneys having slowed or even stopped. The expert who has his name and credentials "out there" will suffer less in these times. Advertising will keep a stream of business coming in during the slow times, especially if done in conjunction with networking and other forms of marketing.

Some experts are understandably wary of advertising. I see forensic advertising that I consider objectionable, advertising that a skilled attorney could use to impeach an expert witness. On the other hand, the fact that one advertises is not in itself objectionable. Advertising is not the basis of being viewed as a "hired gun." That results, instead, from the prostituting of oneself by shaping the facts and opinions rendered to produce a desired conclusion.

If you are concerned about how you will look when answering questions about advertising your expert services, remember that the attorney cross-examining you is probably listed in local, state, and national bar association publications; Martindale-Hubbell®; local, state, and national legal magazines and newspapers; the Yellow Pages; and his child's athletic booster directory, as was the judge when he practiced law as an attorney! Do not take the questioning personally. Your responses to the questions, rather than the questions themselves, will determine jurors' and even judges' attitude toward you. You should practice maintaining your poise and articulating prepared responses to purposely emotion-loaded questions.

Many successful experts tell me they let questions about their advertising "bother them all the way to the bank." They feel that questions regarding advertising comprise only one of many issues on the cross-examination list, and they answer them simply and truthfully.

My advice is to keep your advertising professional, conservative, and in good taste. You should also read "how-to" expert witness books and attend expert witness conferences and workshops in order to learn techniques for handling cross-examination questions in deposition and in court. After all, the opposing attorney has an obligation to ask every question that might even remotely discredit you to the jury. Sometimes this process takes the form of asking benign questions or questions with benign answers, but in phraseology or a tone of voice that attempts to evoke an emotional response from you. Giving a matter-of-fact answer, using a normal tone of voice in a poised manner of speaking, will defuse such questions.

More often than objectionable advertising, I see advertising that is not cost-effective. Advertising is too costly for you to be careless in your selections. Beware, particularly, of using an advertising agency that is not familiar with the legal market. Ad agencies will almost certainly steer you to run display ads, which are effective for only a small percentage of expert witnesses, and only in specific situations. Agencies love to create display ads, because they tap their creative juices and usually merit large commissions.

HOW MUCH TO SPEND ON ADVERTISING

You will experience greater results from your advertising outlay if you regard it as a long-range investment rather than an immediate expense. Experts' budgets for advertising range from zero to approximately 15% of revenue and occasionally more. In the beginning of your practice, before you have much revenue, advertising is pure investment.

No one can advise you exactly how much to spend on advertising. Although you should notice where your competitors advertise, do not fall into the trap of matching their outlay. Your practice is unique. You may concentrate on other forms of marketing, such as building a superior referral system, or working twice as hard at networking.

Be diligent in asking others what works for them, and learn as you build your practice. It requires investigation and experience to determine what works for your professional practice area, your personality, your geographic region, and your target audience. And, like everything else in life, it can change over time.

TYPES OF ADVERTISING

The most cost-effective advertising for expert witnesses is advertising with an extended shelf life such as resume directories, and advertising that provides frequent and consistent exposure, such as classified ads and Internet advertising. Directory listings are so important that a complete chapter is devoted to them. Internet marketing also is discussed in its own chapter.

Standard advertising is of two primary types – display and classified. It runs in newspapers, magazines, journals, and specialty publications such as jury verdict reports. Display and classified ads are different from each other in both purpose and design.

a) Display Advertising

A display ad must call attention to itself. It is placed, ROP, "run of the paper," amid text. Unlike classified advertising, at which the reader is purposefully looking, display advertising must pull the reader's eye away from the text, so it begins with an attention-getting phrase or picture. A display ad can range from a few inches in size up to a full page or even a double page. Display ads cost from less than $100 for a small ad in a small publication to thousands of dollars. They are usually one-time runs but can be repeated frequently on a continuing contract. Display ads are considered "image advertising" and are not necessarily expected to produce a direct response in the reader, but instead are intended to build awareness and credibility.

Running a display ad regularly can be cost-prohibitive, and a one-shot ad is like shooting with a shotgun, since only about half of the general attorney population are litigators – the primary employers of most experts. Therefore, it is advisable for these experts, when using display advertising, to select limited audience publications, such as magazines specifically for plaintiff lawyers or defense lawyers.

In addition, it frequently makes sense to place a one-time display ad in a special section or pull-out that focuses on a particular type of practice of the law in a bar newspaper or magazine, if your consulting focus is in that branch of the law.

Typically, big companies, such as international accounting firms, run display ads. They have large advertising budgets and a marketing posture not applicable to most other expert witnesses.

You represent the client.
We represent the facts.

Managed Liability Associates — a team of medical, legal and managed care administration professionals knowledgeable and experienced in:

- HMO, PPO
- Insurance and managed care law
- National Accreditation Guidelines
- Medicare and Medicaid
- Federal Employees Health Benefits Program
- ERISA, COBRA, EMTALA, HIPAA
- Qui Tam, False Claims Act

We help you get to the heart of the matter—the real issues involved in the case.

MANAGED LI ABILITY ASSOCIATES

THE MANAGED CARE
LITIGATION EXPERTS

202-585-1811

www.ManagedLiability.com

Designing a Display Ad

Although much analysis and creativity goes into producing a display ad, the form is consistent, whether a full-page ad in a major newspaper or magazine or a small ad in a regional periodical. It is similar to nearly every sermon you have heard or slept through, each of which contained "three points and a prayer." A display ad contains 1) an interest attracting phrase, photo, or graphic, 2) text, usually short, 3) identification of the firm, and 4) a "clincher," such as the slogan of the company, guarantee, or logo.

The most important part of a display ad is the headline. One waste of costly advertising space is to put your name as the headline of a display ad, unless you are really famous or the firm name explicitly states what you do. The headline should grab attention by, e.g., asking a question or promising a benefit relating to the demographics of that publication's readers. The headline might be a graphic or photo or a short line of copy. Photos, especially photos of people, draw attention.

Effective headlines evoke the needs, wants, and desires of the prospect in words or symbols. They convince the reader to read the rest of the ad. In a publication targeted at maritime lawyers, for example, it could be as simple as a graphic or photo of a ship and the line, "Expert in Marine Claims," or as provocative as, "Don't Let Your Case Go Down with the Ship!"

Headline examples:
- Engaging the Expert Early Saves You Money Later.
- Wake Up the Jury!
- Don't Wait until Your Case Crashes in Technology!

The text explains the product or service in terms of its value to the reader. In sales jargon, this is called stating benefits, not just features (your services). The text can also communicate credibility, such as your credentials, length of time spent in your profession, or testimonials from satisfied clients. Remember that you are communicating not just the facts of what you provide or how, but, of more importance, the *value* to the client.

Most display ads should have only a few sentences or lines in the text, and even those should be broken up into paragraphs and/or bullet points. If you must use sentences in a display ad, make them short.

A critical point to remember in designing a display ad, besides writing a seductive headline, is to leave plenty of white space throughout the ad. The reader should be able to glance at the ad and perceive the message without concentrating. If he can do so, he will be more inclined to then read the text.

The third section of a display ad, which is identification of the firm – name and contact information – is an area to watch when dealing with advertising agencies. Some designers find it more artistically pleasing to have the identification information appear insignificant in relation to the text – a classic clash of artistry and business.

For example, an expert witness firm asked me to critique for legal marketing purposes an ad their agency had produced for them to run in *The Wall Street Journal*. Their Web site address, listed at the bottom of the ad, was italicized and was so small that I could hardly read it. I reminded them that, in addition, newsprint could slightly blur the type, almost guaranteeing that the small, italicized line would be illegible when printed.

Most display ads place a "punch" at the end. It can be a credibility statement, such as length of time in business, a guarantee, the slogan of the business, or a logo. A similar ad in a direct mail piece will have a call to action in this area, but a display ad rarely does. This omission of a response request is a part of what classifies a display ad as "image advertising."

Professional Announcement

A hybrid of the display ad is the Professional Announcement. Professional announcements can be published in legal newspapers, magazines, and journals, usually at a lower rate than comparably sized display ads. They attract attention because they are similar to attorneys' announcements. People are naturally curious to find out what is happening with their associates. Even if your announcement is printed in an area of the publication separate from attorney announcements, it is still an effective method at a reasonable cost to bring your firm to the attorneys' attention.

Professional announcements publicize a key event, e.g., opening your practice, the addition of new associates, or the accomplishment of an additional degree or certification. The format is formal, usually stated in the third person. While a sales pitch is inappropriate, you can include a brief statement of your services or expertise along with complete contact information.

You can design an announcement to publish in a legal publication and use the same design for a mail piece. You might even save design costs altogether if the publication provides ad set-up at no cost. Ask them to send you the design after the announcement has run.

b) Classified Advertising

The classified section of a legal periodical is a targeted Yellow Pages, and can be a cost-effective advertising venue for experts. Classified ads are like Yellow Pages in that they are categorized and usually sub-categorized. For instance, an expert witness services page might have a category of Medical and various medical sub-specialties under that title.

If an attorney is looking at the expert witness classified section, he is most likely seeking an expert. As a result, a classified ad does not need to be large or to waste space with an attention-getting phrase or logo or benefits, unless there are ads for several similar firms and the ad needs to stand out from the others. Also, it is more beneficial to run a small ad in every scheduled issue than to run a large ad in every other issue.

Classified Advertisements

Classified ads are sold by the column-inch, number of lines, or number of words. Two of the ads shown illustrate how classified column-inch ads resemble display ads. A two column-inch ad can be either one column wide by two inches tall or two columns wide by one inch tall. If both are offered, draft your ad copy and see which dimension fits the shape of the text. If your ad has a list of items, choose the taller, thinner ad. If your ad has long phrases or clauses, or a long list, choose the wider ad.

Basically, a classified ad contains your name and contact information, a bit of information about what you do (features), and your credentials. Your basic degrees and credentials are adequate for a classified ad, as the interested attorney will request your complete c.v. In most instances, I would omit the address, as most inquirers will respond by phone, fax, or e-mail, and you can use the space for more message.

Classified Advertising — A Long-Term Run

I recommend a minimum of a year for running a classified ad. It is a listing, rather than a consumer advertisement that creates a need. Only after an extended period will you know whether the ad produces business. Litigation is cyclical. Like most people, attorneys and judges do not like to work when it is extremely cold or hot, or during holidays and other times when their children are out of school. Issues such as tort reform or a period of low jury awards also influence the number of cases filed. You need to advertise throughout these up and down times. You should no more remove your listing during a slow season than you would periodically take down the For Sale sign from your front yard.

One year I worked in my office at *Texas Lawyer* every day of the holidays except Christmas Day, catching up on paperwork and organizing for the coming year. During that time, I received three or four calls from attorneys looking for expert witnesses, one on Christmas Eve! After I teased them saying that I expected them to be away skiing, they told me that they too were catching up on administrative tasks and getting organized for the new year.

Dr. Harvey Loomstein of Biotech Institute in Dallas remarked that he received considerably more business from his classified ad in *Texas Lawyer* newspaper in the third and fourth years than in the first two years. When I queried him, his conclusion was that attorneys became accustomed to seeing the ad, perhaps when they were looking for other medical specialties or just scanning, and later recalled his ad when they needed his services.

Do not frequently change your ad, particularly the size and shape of it. People recall subliminally what they have seen – a shape, a general position on the page, a particular font. If you alter the emphasis of your practice, or due to issues before the courts it becomes advisable to change the way you express certain terms in your industry, then modify the ad. Do not change it simply because *you* are tired of it. Think about how easily you recall billboards that have never changed and ads that run in the same spot in a publication for many years.

PROOFREADING YOUR AD

In addition to proofing any advertising you plan to run, ask the advertising representative and others to proof it. First, check for content. Do not ask whether they like it – ask what it says to them. Try to determine if the message comes through. Get their overall impression and also what they recall after seeing the ad. Then check for grammar and typographical errors.

Verify the accuracy of the ad when it is first published and in every issue thereafter. The publisher should send you a tear sheet of each issue in which it runs. If you find an error or it appears in a different spot than agreed, most publications are fair about issuing credit. No matter how long your advertising has been running, check it every issue. Stuff happens. If you discover that an error has run for three issues and you are just then reporting it, the publication is liable only for the most recent issue.

PURCHASING ADVERTISING

If you ask a publication representative for the publication's circulation number, he may respond that the subscription number is X and readership is Y. This is not sales doubletalk. Readership, also known as the pass-along rate, is significant. Many publishers even hire independent audit firms to survey their readers' pass-along numbers so that they can quote a verified number. Large law firms buy a few copies of publications, list five or ten associates' names on each copy, and pass them around.

Ask for the demographics of the publication. If a very small percentage of a particular legal publication uses expert witnesses, you may still want to advertise in it, but adjust your budget allocation accordingly.

Attorneys are as cost conscious as other business people and more so if they are working on contingency. Therefore, for most experts, advertising outside their geographic region is not cost-effective. The exception is if your field is very narrow or your credentials or experience unique enough to justify being hired by an attorney in a distant state. If so, contract for a package deal to advertise in legal newspapers and directories that are part of national chains. Set up a toll-free number to increase your chance of speaking with a prospective client before he might eliminate you because of a perceived disadvantage of distance. You might convince him that you are the best consultant for the case regardless of your location.

Frequency discounts are usually available on both classified and display advertising. This means that the more frequently you agree to advertise, the less each run of the ad costs. Calculate the math carefully. The value of the discount might not increase in equal increments. A six-month contract might offer a substantial rate discount over running only three months, whereas the per issue rate on a nine-month contract might not be substantially better than the six-month rate. Even though the recommended length of time to try a publication is one year, there might be one that you want to try for a shorter period, so verify the incremental rate of discount.

Short-rate is a term used to explain the penalty for discontinuing advertising during a discounted contract period. If you agree to advertise for a year at an annual discounted rate and quit halfway through, the publication can recalculate the six months already run at the published rate for a half-year contract and charge you the difference. In many cases, the short-rate is high enough to warrant simply going ahead and completing the remainder of the contract as scheduled.

SPECIALTY ADVERTISING

Some individuals and firms offering their services to attorneys give away advertising specialties such as writing pens, calendars, and coffee mugs with their names on them. I am not convinced of the value of experts doing so. If you give away specialty items, select your item and message imprint carefully, lest you look "sales-y" and unprofessional.

If you want to invest in gifts for appropriate occasions such as holidays, you might buy treats such as candy or nuts, and put your name and number on the packages, for the "gatekeepers" of your principal clients and prospective clients. The secretary or paralegal is often in control of your ability to contact the attorney (and might be consulted for an opinion about you).

COMMENT

As a professional engaging in litigation work, you are intelligent, educated, communicative, professional in your demeanor, and perhaps slightly conservative. Your advertising should reflect who you are. Consult marketing and advertising books to learn more about advertising, but remember that not all points are applicable to your legal market niche – some are appropriate only for a general consumer market.

CAUTION

Your advertising will be shown to you someday in court for comments before a jury. Consider your image and ensure that your advertising is consistent with that image.

DIRECTORY LISTINGS

Why Some Work and Some Do Not

CHAPTER TWELVE GUIDE

- Types of Expert Witness Directories
  - Expert Witness Directory Only
  - Expert Witness Directory Combined with Other Reference Material
  - Courthouse Guide
  - Attorney Directory with Expert Witness Section
  - Periodic Expert Witness Directory Inside a Magazine or Newspaper
- Directory Listing Costs
- Your Listing Information
- Directory Format
- Directory Advertising Outside Your Region
- Consistency in Listing

Listing in expert witness directories is one of the most cost-effective ways to inform large numbers of attorneys of your qualifications. Although all of your marketing is open to scrutiny, some experts consider placing a resume in a directory more acceptable than display or classified advertising. Print directories have a long shelf life and, in fact, seem to never be thrown away. Experts have received calls from directories printed years earlier.

This chapter addresses print directories; Internet expert witness directories are covered in the Internet marketing chapter.

TYPES OF EXPERT WITNESS DIRECTORIES

a) Expert witness directory only

The most effective directory in which to promote your services is an expert witness directory that exists solely as a source for lawyers or insurance professionals to locate expert witnesses. Attorneys and law libraries keep them on file for reference and access them when they need an expert. At times they even consult directories when they know which expert they want, but do not have contact information.

b) Expert witness directory combined with other reference material

Publications such as jury verdict reports, also containing expert witness listings, have not proven to be as effective as publications containing only expert witnesses. The message is diffused. Although it might occur to the attorney to access the book to find experts, he may consider the book only as a source for the other information, and not as a resource to find experts.

c) Courthouse guide

Courthouse guides are reference books typically used by legal secretaries and other legal support personnel. They list telephone numbers for the various courts and judges, maps of the courthouse and surrounding area, and a section listing legal vendors including expert witnesses. The use of these books to locate expert witnesses is minimal, although they can work well for true "litigation support" vendors such as court reporters. *The Legal Pages of New Jersey* seems to also work for experts. It serves as a reminder that there are exceptions, and you should thoroughly investigate all promotional avenues in your area.

d) Attorney directory with expert witness section

An increasing number of attorney directories, both association membership and commercial, include an advertising section for legal vendors of various kinds and, in some instances, a separate section just for expert witnesses. Unfortunately, the more well-known the directory is as a source for attorneys to find other attorneys, the less chance there is that an attorney will consider this kind of directory as a source of experts. A few state or regional directories of only plaintiff or defense attorneys, e.g., the *Texas Trial Lawyers Association Membership Directory*, are exceptions. For the advertising section to work for the advertiser, the association or commercial publisher needs to educate its members to use the section as a resource to find expert witnesses.

e) Periodic expert witness directory inside a magazine or newspaper

Certain legal magazines and newspapers periodically run an extra section called an *Expert Witness Directory*. This is not to be confused with display or regular, consistent classified advertising in these periodicals, or with a freestanding expert witness directory. The publication may not be kept to be used as a source of expert witnesses, but instead may be thrown away after the publication is read. If you decide to advertise in this kind of temporary directory (and I occasionally recommend doing so), pay accordingly, because the rate should match the brief exposure.

DIRECTORY LISTING COSTS

The rate of a directory listing depends primarily upon the number of copies distributed and the method of distribution.

The most effective distribution for the expert witness is for the directories to be sent free of charge to attorneys. The books can be mailed or handed out at attorney meetings. A directory that is sold to attorneys will have an unreliable circulation. A notable exception is the *Forensic Services Directory*, which has been published and sold to attorneys for twenty-two years.

If directories are distributed to an entire state bar membership, a large portion of the copies are virtually wasted. Litigators only comprise about fifty percent of attorneys, and many types of expert witnesses are hired primarily by litigators, both plaintiff and defense.

In short, the ideal expert witness directory is free to attorneys and with most of the copies distributed to litigators.

Annual rates for directory listings will range from about $250 to $1,000. When determining value, the questions you should ask are:

- Is the directory solely an expert witness source, or is it used for other purposes?
- How many years has the directory been published?
- How many copies are published each year?
- Are the directories free to attorneys?
- Are they distributed to all types of attorneys, or only litigators, or at least mostly litigators?
- Are any other benefits attached, such as free or discounted advertising on the Internet, or free attorney referrals?
- What is the directory's renewal rate? Does a reasonable majority of advertisers achieve sufficient results to list year after year?

Call current advertisers to determine their level of satisfaction. If you do not have a copy of the directory, ask the representative to fax you a page or two so that you can call advertisers. Do not be intimidated by cries of privacy invasion – these books are in the public domain.

If the directory is long-standing or is published by a well-known publishing company, you can write a check or give a credit card number with confidence. If the directory is a first issue and is being published by a company with whom you are not familiar, insist on paying upon publication. All publications must have a first issue, but advertisers should not have to take the up-front financial risk.

YOUR LISTING INFORMATION

Your submission to a print directory may be a resume or short biography, a classified listing, or a hybrid, e.g., a large, boxed classified ad that looks almost like a display ad.

If the directory contains classified listings, put your name and contact information, areas of expertise and services, and as much about your credentials as you can fit into the space.

If the directory is in a resume format, include some or all of the following:
- Name, address, appropriate numbers
- Areas of expertise
- Services offered of interest to attorneys
- Education
- Professional experience
- Professional qualifications and affiliations
- Honors and awards
- Publications, speeches, media presentations
- Geographical limitations, if any

I do not recommend stating your rates in directories. Publishing your rate might disqualify you in advance to an attorney who, if he spoke with you, might decide that your services are worth exceeding his budget plans. Published rates also provide ammunition to the attorney cross-examining you. Furthermore, raising your rates is simpler if you have not published them. You may say something like "Rates and terms available upon request," or "Initial discussion at no cost."

Beware of putting bogus diplomate status or "Who's Who" awards from organizations of interest only to the persons "selected," (read: "paid for a copy of the book"). It cannot be stated too often: Everything is potential material for cross-examination.

You might have an option to list well-known or successful award cases in which you were instrumental. This could be advantageous, but list cases cautiously, and with permission. Remember that directory contents are open to public view.

Since a directory resume is not your official *c.v.*, you can include a bit of self-promotion, but remain careful and conservative.

DIRECTORY FORMAT

Your listing may be placed within a field of knowledge such as Engineering or a sub-category of Automotive Engineering, or perhaps an application of specialty, such as Accident Investigation or Reconstruction.

Your resume may be placed alphabetically and then cross-referenced to terms an attorney would use to find you, similar to the three terms above.

Ideally you should use a previous directory for reference as well as a list of indexes from which to choose your categories. You need to consider the indexing system and how the book is arranged, and carefully select indexes for your maximum benefit.

DIRECTORY ADVERTISING OUTSIDE YOUR REGION

If your credentials are unique, your specialty particularly narrow, or your experience so special that you are likely to be engaged by a distant attorney, directories are the most cost-effective nationwide advertising you can utilize, other than the Internet. In the expert witness directories published by American Lawyer Media, now the National Law Journal, an expert receives an ascending discount factor for each additional regional directory in which he lists. For the right expert, this is a bargain. For others, multiple directory listings might be wasted money. To many of my clients who ask whether they should advertise outside their region, I respond, "Bloom where you are planted." Remember the qualifying terms at the beginning of this paragraph.

CONSISTENCY IN LISTING

One reason directory listings are a good option for experts is that you experience a year's results before you choose to renew or not renew. Most advertising should be run for a period of a year in order to ascertain its effectiveness through natural seasonal and other fluctuations. Furthermore, your results should increase in succeeding years. Attorneys who regularly use a particular directory may not need you this year but might recall that you were in a previous directory and look for you in the next issue.

C O M M E N T

On occasion attorneys consult "expert" (not "expert witness") directories that list people who are authorities in their fields, who might or might not have experience in litigation support. Since this listing might be a long shot from a legal business standpoint, your cost-effectiveness risk decision on listing would depend on whether you think that it might also generate business from sources other than legal.

INTERNET

Experts in Cyberspace

CHAPTER THIRTEEN GUIDE

- E-mail
  - Choosing an Internet Service Provider for E-Mail
- Your Web Site
  - Selecting a Domain Name
  - Registering Your Domain Name
  - Hosting
  - Designing Your Web Site
  - Content of Your Web Site
  - Positioning Your Web Site
    - Search Engines
    - Pay-Per-Click Search Engine Advertising
  - Marketing Your Web Site
- Advertising in Internet Expert Witness Directories
  - How to Choose Internet Expert Witness Directories
- Internet Marketing Budget
  - Internet Expert Witness Directories
  - Moderate Cost Internet Marketing
  - Customized Internet Marketing Strategy

The Expert Witness Marketing Book

꒰ꔷ꒱Not that long ago, Cyberspace was billed as the New Frontier and it has indeed created vast opportunities to reach previously unimaginable numbers of people. The Internet makes communication available not only to more people than would be possible through only print advertising and other media, but also to people who might be inaccessible through any other means.

Marketing on the Internet, however, is not simply creating a Web site and waiting for attorneys to find it. Creating a Web site is recommended for most experts, but only as one facet of a complete Internet marketing strategy.

An expert who is likely to be sought by attorneys throughout the country needs to create a Web site. On the other hand, having a Web site is not critical for an expert whose target prospect group is mostly local and regional. In this case, the expert needs to include Internet marketing in his overall promotional plans, but instead of creating a Web site, he can first choose other activities, e.g., devoting appreciable effort in personal networking with attorney groups in his area. He might consider building a Web site later.

More and more, the public expects a professional to have a Web site much as he is expected to have a business card. In addition, even if a Web site is not constructed primarily for the purpose of attracting new business, making the expert's qualifications easily accessible to a prospect with whom he is already in contact is advantageous.

The expert witness should consider listing his services on Internet expert witness directories regardless of whether he creates a Web site. Attorneys use directories as a quick and convenient resource to locate experts and view their qualifications.

This chapter will explore, on a basic level, setting up a Web site and define terms for the individual who has little or no knowledge of the Internet. Internet expert witness directories will also be discussed. Sending promotional information by e-mail is discussed in the direct mail chapter.

E-MAIL

You should now have e-mail service. E-mail is available 24 hours a day, provides instantaneous communication, and is inexpensive. A growing number of the population assumes e-mail availability and considers it a burden to send posted "snail" mail. Just as the fax machine greatly enhanced and sped up communication 15 or 20 years ago, e-mail has taken communication another giant step forward.

Your e-mail address should be professional and simple. Avoid casual addresses, e.g., sundaygolfer@__. Your name or a shortened version, or words relating to your profession, e.g., marineexpert@__, are the best choices. Do not add a string of numbers after your name. They make recalling your address more difficult.

Remember that you have the option of changing your e-mail address to reflect your domain name when you create a Web site. Instead of rjwatson@[ISP], you can use rjwatson@[domain-name].

Choosing an Internet Service Provider for E-mail

If you travel frequently, you may want to use a national or international ISP such as Earthlink, Southwestern Bell, or AT&T. Providers such as these have accounts set up in the major cities, whereby you can dial up a local access number from their directory rather than using a toll-free number and then paying perhaps 18 cents a minute. Investigate your prospective ISP before signing up. If you do not travel often, a local, less costly ISP might be a better choice.

YOUR WEB SITE

You will hear the terms, "home page" and "Web site," used interchangeably. In fact, only the first page of your Web site is the home page, which is what people see when they first come to your site. The home page and any succeeding pages comprise your Web site.

Selecting a Domain Name

The URL, or Uniform Resource Locator, or Web address, is also called a domain name (www.domainname.com). Select a domain name that reflects who you are or what you do and is easy to remember. You can check name availability on any of the registration services sites, such as www.register.com and www.verisign.com (formerly Network Solutions). The .com version is preferable, and second choice would be .net, although .biz and .info are also acceptable.

Consider that the name you choose will appear on all of your materials and will be cited often in conversation. Do not select something that is too long, too complicated, or too cute.

Yahoo! says that hyphenated names fare better in searches, as the words show individually for searches; for instance, www.metal-roofs.com is better than www.metalroofs.com. The other search engines have not issued similar advice, and proper search engine optimization steps on the site should make that choice unnecessary. A hyphenated name might be a better choice than having to choose another, less descriptive name if your original name has already been taken. One drawback, however, is that a hyphenated name might be more difficult to remember and type. Stay alert for information such as this, as Internet issues and concerns evolve constantly.

Registering Your Domain Name

Register your domain name with a domain name registration company such as www.register.com. A common rate is $70 for two years, with an annual renewal of $35, although some companies charge less and most companies occasionally run promotional, discounted rates. Register a name even if you are not ready to build a Web site. Thousands of names are registered every day. You would not want to regret in future years that you had not reserved a particular name. The registration service, for a small fee, will "park" (hold) your domain name without a Web site. I do not recommend publicizing your domain name and setting up an "Under Construction" page on the Internet unless you really are building a Web site soon. Just let the service hold the name for you until you are ready.

Although the preferred suffix is still .com (pronounced "dot com"), you might want to purchase other suffixes just to prevent other people from having the same domain name as yours but with a different suffix. If you purchase additional domain names, have them "pointed" to your site so that if someone types in the alternate suffix, he will still arrive at your site.

If you are planning to create a Web site, your host can handle the name registration for you. This procedure is easier than registering with a registration company and then having to move the domain name from being "parked" on the registration site to the host site.

Hosting

You will need a host for your Web site on the World Wide Web, which is that section of the Internet open to the public for personal and business use. Other areas of the Internet include e-mail and certain military and scientific data sources not available to everyone.

The host is the company with a communication line to the Internet, that is, a computer that runs 24 hours a day, and someone who knows how to keep the computer running. If you use a commercial Web site hosting service to host your Web site with your personal domain name, you can put your permanent domain address on your business card and stationery without being concerned about future changes. Even if you switch hosting services, your address will not change.

Placing your Web site on someone else's domain, such as that of your e-mail ISP or an Internet expert witness directory, will be less costly, but you may not have the option of keeping the same Web address when moving your Web site to another host should you choose to. Another factor to consider is how professional and memorable your domain name will be; some of these arrangements include their name along with yours in the domain name. Registering your own domain name and using a commercial hosting service will allow you to have a concise name that others can easily recall.

Be wary of small, discount rate hosts. Although the large technology companies are sometimes time-consuming to reach, their customer service departments are available 24 hours a day. Some of the large hosts are Interland, interland.com; Earthlink, earthlink.net (for simple/basic sites); and Innerhost, innerhost.com. These hosts are examples, not necessarily recommendations. Ask your friends and associates for recommendations, based on factors such as technical help and customer service.

Designing Your Web Site

Designing a Web site is similar to outlining your resume or preparing a brochure about your services, consisting of both composition and technical design. You may be capable of doing one or the other, both, or neither. If you feel that you can compose and arrange the information yourself for the best marketing advantage and ensure that the content is appropriate and acceptable for legal marketing, at least have the pages proofread by someone else before you send them to a Web site designer. Even though some of them are whizzes at the technical part, their English/grammar/punctuation skills are often inadequate. Look at several Web sites, and you will see many that need a good dose of "the teacher's red pencil."

A person who is very computer-oriented could possibly build his own site using software such as Microsoft FrontPage or Trellix, or an online site builder from Netscape or Yahoo!. Some of the do-it-yourself Web site software utilizes templates, which turn out a "cookie cutter" site. This can make updating and revising the site difficult.

For most experts, creating a Web site is a task best outsourced. Furthermore, knowing how to design and then load sites onto the Internet is not the same as knowing and understanding search engine optimization. Many attractive, effective-looking Web sites have little chance of being found by the search engines.

You can have a Web site developed by a custom Web site designer, by various Internet expert witness directories, or perhaps by your Internet Service Provider. A custom Web site designer might be more objective about your individual Web site than a designer from an Internet-only expert witness directory, but few understand legal marketing principles. An expert witness directory designer would more likely have knowledge of legal marketing, but might use a "cookie-cutter" approach for the experts in that directory. A designer from a general ISP might have the necessary technical skills but might not understand the unique legal marketing posture of your site.

The optimum procedure is to look for designers' names on Web sites you like and to ask for recommendations from other professionals, especially expert witnesses, who have sites. Confirm that the sites produce prospects, rather than just look attractive and perhaps contain a lot of information.

CAUTION

When you contract with someone to design and/or host your Web site, read the agreement carefully. The technical writing needs to be your property in the event that you wish to later move to another host or designer. It is imperative that you ask for and keep a copy of the html code, graphics, and any other documents or files created by the designer for the site, along with access data – FTP information, username, and password for the site. Experts have paid for site design and later decided to revise the site through another designer, only to find that they did not even own their own site.

Content of Your Web Site

Content is king. The information and its presentation on your site drive the success of the site. It is a text-based environment, where content, not graphics, determines the style.

The pages should contain your resume, your photograph (relatively current), areas of specialty, and the services you perform. Photos relating to your area of work add interest and build understanding. Make contact information easy to find. The best method is to place it on every page of the Web site, rather than creating a Contact page.

Some experts put their entire *c.v.*'s on their sites. A summary, such as a "Brief Biographical Sketch," is preferable for two reasons:

1) The most ignored marketing principle, and one of the most important, is that advertising should be designed to elicit contact, not to give the prospect all the information he needs, rendering contact unnecessary. Nothing, not even your own advertising, can convey the value of using your services as well as you can. Leave a reason for the prospect to talk to you before making a decision to eliminate you.

2) The continuation of your professional life creates additions to and changes in items on your *c.v.* Making those changes on paper is easier than on your Web site.

An expert witness site is not a "surfing" site. Attorneys and their paralegals search for expert witnesses, they do not just "happen upon" them. This makes the design parameters different from a consumer-oriented site. If you are creating the site specifically to attract attorneys and possibly insurers, avoid the "bells & whistles" that might enhance a consumer-oriented site. Even a great deal of educational material, such as white papers you have written, adds unnecessary clutter. In particular, avoid gimmicks that make the site slow to develop, such as complex or animated graphics. An attorney prospect might not have time to wait, or he might leave the site because the wait is annoying.

Despite popular advice to arrange multiple links to and from your site to increase search results, be careful of to whom and to what you are linked. Your credibility is at stake. Also, ensure that even a link to a credible, associated site within your profession does not "take the viewer off the site," i.e., make sure he can click on the Back button and return to your site.

The challenge is to make the site accommodating for as many of the major search engines as possible and have your site near the top of their search results. For instance, certain search engines will de-list a site for using words on the page or in the code in an excessively repetitive manner (erroneously recommended by some people to attract searches). Strategies in both composition and technical design can optimize search engine results. The text can be arranged to be both user-friendly and well positioned for search engines. If you do not know how search engines access information, getting professional help to create your Web site, as well as in composing and programming the information, is a worthwhile investment.

Creating an informative, attractive Web site is not enough. To ensure that people searching for your type of expertise find your site, you must:

- Compose the text and design the site itself to be search-engine friendly.
- Follow search engine optimization guidelines in coding your information.
- Submit the site to search engines and Internet directories.
- List your information, including a link to your Web site, on several Internet expert witness directories.

Search Engines

A search engine is a database of Web sites created by a program called a "spider" or "crawler," which runs automatically and searches the Web, cataloging Web sites by their content. A directory is an index created by humans, with sites that are submitted, reviewed, and then categorized.

You or your designer should register your site with search engines, such as:

- Lycos – www.Lycos.com
- Altavista – www.AltaVista.com
- Google – www.Google.com
- HotBot – www.HotBot.com (at the time of this writing not accepting submissions)
- FAST Search – www.alltheweb.com
- MSN Search – www.search.msn.com

and at least two directories: The Open Directory Project (www.dmoz.com), which powers the core directory services for the Web's largest and most popular search engines and portals, and Yahoo! Directory (www.yahoo.com), the oldest major Internet directory. Yahoo! charges $299 per year, but is worth the investment because it drives the most Internet traffic. At the time of this writing, The Open Directory Project and the search engines listed are free to register. Lycos currently charges a minimal fee, around $30.

For online information and tips on search engine submission, see www.searchenginewatch.com.

There are also services that offer to register sites with huge numbers of search engines – hundreds or even thousands – but no great results have been reported so far. Since you do not know what sites yours might end up being linked to in such an arrangement, this procedure is somewhat akin to having your telephone number posted on the restroom door.

Other services guarantee that your site will come up in the top ten listings of the most popular search engines for a rate of approximately $1,000 per year or more. One method is to renew the search engine registrations and change the site contents on a regular basis to attract the search engines that rate sites by how often they are modified. Consumer businesses that are mostly dependent on search engine results employ these companies as standard practice.

Fortunately, with proper design of the site, registering with search engines, and listing with Internet expert witness directories, expert witnesses normally do not have to incur this additional expense.

Pay-Per-Click Search Engine Advertising

A new way to push your site to the top of search engine results is to bid on your keywords against other search engine registrants, and then pay for each resulting click. You can find information about this procedure at Overture, www.overture.com, and Google, www.adwords.google.com/select/main.

A few of the Internet expert witness directories have bid on a few categories, but this could become cost prohibitive for them due to their large number of categories. With proper search engine positioning, individual expert witnesses have not yet had to use this method.

Marketing Your Web Site

Drive traffic to your site. List your domain address on your business card, stationery, and all advertising. On your e-mail create a signature form which includes your Web site address.

Creating a Web site or revising an existing one is a good reason to mail a professional announcement to your established mailing list. Invite people to visit your site.

ADVERTISING IN INTERNET EXPERT WITNESS DIRECTORIES

An expert witness should list his services in Internet expert witness directories, whether or not he has a Web site. As of now, no one has yet surveyed legal professionals as to their preference for going to an Internet expert witness directory site as opposed to searching with a keyword on the Web. As many experts can attest, listings on Internet expert witness directories do result in business. Logically, if attorneys know of a comprehensive, user-friendly directory, they will take this short cut.

The two types of Internet expert witness directories are those that are a source of expert witnesses exclusively and those that are "attorney sites." Examples of expert witness resource-only directories are www.expertpages.com, www.experts.com (formerly The Noble Group), www.ewitness.com, and www.jurispro.com. Examples of attorney resource sites that include an expert witness directory as one of several offerings are www.findlaw.com, www.law.com, and www.lawinfo.com.

Internet expert witness directories offer a range of services, from a simple listing of your name, contact information, and specialty in a categorized list, to extensive options such as including papers you have written and your voice recording for the attorney to hear, and even to resources for the expert witnesses themselves such as Web site development, chat rooms, and technical research resources.

How to Choose Internet Expert Witness Directories

The first factor in choosing directories is that searching the directory should be free to the attorney. There are too many free sources of expert witnesses for the attorney to pay to use one. Along with being free to the attorney, a directory should not require him to register on the site, as he could become annoyed and decide to use a different directory.

An important determinant is whether the directory markets its site in ways other than the Internet. In 1999, I went against the tide by saying that an Internet site should not depend solely on search engines for traffic but must also market itself in print and other media. In 2001 I felt vindicated when advertisements for Amazon.com began arriving inside my Sunday newspaper!

ExpertPages.com, for example, is an Internet expert witness directory that I recommend because the site is advertised in legal publications, and the staff exhibits at large legal conferences. Even though ExpertPages.com is slightly more costly than similar directories, the traffic generated for the site by marketing outside the Internet creates proportionate value for most advertisers.

In addition to exhibiting at large legal conventions, JurisPro.com, built by practicing attorneys, works with law firms to electronically import member information directly into the internal network of a number of the largest law firms in the country. JurisPro.com also sends information about their experts to the top 250 law firms.

Earlier recommendations, including mine, were to ask for the number of visitors (not hits) a site received per month. Hits are the number of pieces of information and/or graphics delivered to a user. The total from one page view could be fifteen or twenty or many more. A visitor is the one individual accessing that page view. A unique visitor is an individual visiting the site only once or for the first time within a defined period, so a tally of unique visitors would be the number of *different* people who visited the site within a defined period.

You have heard the saying that "figures do not lie, but liars figure." Well, I have become convinced that the statistics explained in the above paragraph are easily massaged and so inconsistently interpreted that they are not a reliable basis for choosing a directory. A particularly unhelpful statistic is how many hits an "attorney site" receives, with no distinction made as to how many of them are for the expert witness directory section. Furthermore, since you want a site where attorneys know to go to look for expert witnesses whenever they need them, the number of unique visitors is not a relevant issue.

A few directories contract to include their expert witness listings on the sites of Westlaw® and LexisNexis™, the primary Internet legal research sites. This is a valuable benefit due to the large numbers of attorneys who subscribe to these services.

To determine whether to list in a particular directory, first ask:
- How the directory brings attorneys to the site.
- Number of experts listed. (They may not tell you; if not, you can estimate relative size by comparing a few disciplines in the directory to other directories.)
- Retention (renewal) rate for experts.

A directory with few experts will be less attractive to attorneys and also will not provide the revenue necessary for the directory to market the site. Also, if the directory only has experts from a particular geographic area, it is reasonable to expect that the site is promoted primarily to attorneys in just that area.

In addition to asking the directory staff for the retention rate, call four or five people in the directory and ask for their opinion of the site. Selecting experts in different specialties from yours, who would therefore not consider themselves your competitors, will probably result in at least a couple who will give you a fair evaluation of the directory.

Is the directory user-friendly? Although indexing every single term applicable to every discipline would be impractical, put yourself in the place of the attorney, who knows very little about your profession – How will he search? Many years ago the first expert witness referral request I received was from an attorney who said, "I'm looking for a guy who can do a scapula injection." I correctly surmised that since a scapula is bone, he needed an orthopedist. But the attorney did not know that. That incident serves as my reminder that attorneys know the law, not the disciplines of their expert witnesses.

Look at the organization of the site. Is a search process offered, or simply a list of categories? Even if the site does not provide a Boolean search (search of keywords), which is the ideal, the movement from a main category down through sub-categories should be logical. One directory, for example, has no search process or even a category/sub-category system, but rather lists all of the experts in alphabetical order, which is essentially worthless.

If the contact information for the experts is not shown, the site is not a directory, but a referral service. This means that the service either charges for finding the expert for the attorney or adds its fees to the expert's rate. See the chapter on referral services for a full description.

Enter the search terms applicable to your services on a major search engine and notice which expert witness directories show up. Although all of the factors listed above should be weighed, determining which directories have already positioned themselves with your applicable search terms is one place to start in the selection process.

INTERNET MARKETING BUDGET
Internet Expert Witness Directories

If a directory listing costs approximately $300–$500 or less (to come up under any state selected), and the directory markets the site in print, at legal conferences, or in other ways beyond search engine submissions, try a year's listing. Because you should list in several directories, I would not recommend listing in one that costs more than $300–$500 unless you know that other experts have received attorneys calls that they can trace to that directory.

Beware of paying a higher rate to an Internet expert witness directory due to features that you do not need or will not utilize. The key elements are the listing of your basic information, effective marketing of the site to attorneys, and user-friendliness to the attorney searching for an expert witness. In the current, highly competitive market of directories, some are offering "bells & whistles" that might not be essential to an attorney's finding, choosing and contacting you.

Moderate Cost Internet Marketing

- Sign up for e-mail service to make contacting you easy for prospects.
- List with Internet expert witness directories.
- Take advantage of creating a free or inexpensive Web site on one of the Internet expert witness directories. (Note that the stated, low rate may not include Internet positioning of your site for search engines.)

Customized Internet Marketing Strategy

Contracting with a Web site development service that also does marketing in media besides the Internet is worthwhile for the individual or firm for whom the Internet is likely to be a major source of business. Such firms not only design your site and position it for optimum advantage on the Internet, but also integrate your Web site into an overall marketing strategy. The Web site can be simple, but should be focused. The cost for composition and design and Internet positioning might be approximately $2,000. You might also want professional help if you have or want to build a Web site for your non-legal business and want just a page or two for your legal consulting practice. You want attorneys to be able to find your site, and also to ensure that the integration of the legal data is tasteful and appropriate.

∿ The Internet is now an integral part of our culture. If you have not used computers much, it is imperative that you familiarize yourself with their various uses, especially e-mail and simple Internet access. At a minimum, list in Internet expert witness directories and reserve your domain name for the future. To take maximum advantage of the Internet as a marketing tool, build a Web site and market that site.

CAUTION

A printout of your Web site, as well as Internet expert witness directory listings and print advertising, may someday be shown in court for comments before a jury. Make your site professional looking. Do not be cute or flamboyant. Consider what adjectives could be applied to describe it to the jury. If they go beyond "comprehensive," "helpful," and "professional," your presentation is probably in bad form for an expert witness/consultant and may come back to haunt you. Remind yourself that although this is business, it is legal business. The attorney is looking for your credentials, not entertainment.

INSURANCE INDUSTRY

Another Potential Source of Business

CHAPTER FOURTEEN GUIDE

- Overview
- What the Insurance Representative Wants
- Contacting Insurance Professionals
  - Advertising
  - Networking
  - Referrals
- The Insurance Company's Attorney
- Opportunities for Insurance Work
  - Getting Paid for IMEs
- Comments Regarding Working for Insurance Companies

↩️Work for experts can come directly or indirectly from the insurance industry as well as the legal community. An insurance company is a party in many cases, usually as defense. Areas involved include personal injury, product liability, environmental, medical malpractice, disability, and Workers' Compensation.

OVERVIEW

The insurance company often uses the services of an expert to address issues of cause and origin of the accident or other event, cause and extent of injury or impairment, and the likelihood of negligence or malpractice having occurred, and then settles without litigation. The overwhelming majority of insured claims are settled before they reach the courts.

There are more than 2,000 property and casualty insurance companies in the United States, ranging from a single claims office to a large company with 1,000 claims offices. Over the past few years almost all of the major insurance companies have made a concerted effort to develop large phone centers for claims handling. Whereas, historically, the function was grounded in local and even neighborhood claims offices, the current thrust is toward major offices handling all of the claims for an entire state or several states.

Additionally, many large companies in the United States self-insure. Their risk management structure becomes, for all purposes, an insurance company. The analysis and settlement activity is usually out-sourced to a third party administrator (TPA). Although TPA's usually work for self-insured companies they also sometimes work for insurance companies. TPA's can be a source of business, but, in most cases, they bid for the work, and their ability or desire to spend money for claims investigation is limited.

Another potential employer in the insurance field for expert consultants is the independent adjuster or independent adjuster company, with several adjusters or even several claims offices. IA's, too, are working for someone else, e.g., insurance companies and third party administrators. In order for the expert to get paid the IA has to obtain firm approval from his client to retain the expert's services. Verify that the adjuster has that approval.

WHAT THE INSURANCE REPRESENTATIVE WANTS

~ The insurer wants an expert, independent opinion as to what happened and the extent of potential loss. He wants a report that is thorough, accurate, complete, and professionally sound, in language that he and others outside of your profession can understand. Your report card grade will depend on promptness, clarity of the working product, and a bill that does not contain any surprises, as well as the quality of your actual work.

CONTACTING INSURANCE PROFESSIONALS

Books that contain the names and addresses of insurance companies and adjusters all over the country are available. The difficulty lies in determining the right person to contact. The decision-maker may be the adjuster, the head of the claims department, the company's in-house counsel, or the outside attorney. Other titles for in-house counsel are corporate counsel and staff counsel; the head of the Legal Department is sometimes called general counsel. Attempting to identify the decision-maker is time-consuming, frustrating, and sometimes futile.

Some insurance companies and adjusters maintain a "stable" of experts they use regularly and are not open to new prospects. One litigation attorney told me that the insurance company he represents calls theirs a "panel" of experts. In contrast, opposing counsel at trial will frequently try to discredit the testimony of the insurance company's "regulars" as being biased. As a result, the insurance company might rotate experts from time to time.

Large engineering consulting companies have a staff person whose job is to "wine and dine" insurance people so their firm will get the opportunity to join or remain in the "stable." Increasingly, though, many insurance companies forbid employees to accept gifts or even a meal, in order to maintain an appearance of neutrality.

Titles of prospective insurance clients include, among others, Claims Specialist, Claims Representative, Claims Adjuster, Property Adjuster, Casualty Adjuster, Workers' Compensation Adjuster, Safety Adjuster, Senior Adjuster of any of the areas above, or Manager or Supervisor of Property, Casualty, or Liability.

In addition to the difficulty of determining whom to contact, be aware that the contact person may not be the primary buyer. The need for expert services almost always arises at the adjuster level, but approval for the assignment will probably come from a supervisor or manager whose orientation may reside largely in cost consideration. Therefore, if rule number one in marketing to insurance people is to research and verify the contact person (before spending money on materials such as postage), rule number two would be to narrowly define and contract the scope of services, at least until a working relationship is established.

To find third party administrator firms, look on the Internet. Some are listed on the Buyers Guide page of The Professional Insurance Marketing Association site at www.pima-assn.org. The Web site for the Society of Professional Benefit Administrators (employee benefit TPA firms and stop-loss service partners), http://users.erols.com/spba/, states that this organization does not provide opportunities to reach its members.

Advertising

The National Directory of Expert Witnesses, published by Claims Providers of America, is distributed to insurance companies as well as law firms and law libraries. The rate is quite reasonable, and your listing is immediately published online and appears in the next print directory. This is a well-established directory.

Both the *SEAK National Directory of Independent Medical Examiners*™ and the *SEAK National Directory of Medical Experts*™ are distributed to insurance company case managers as well as to trial attorneys. These publications offer a money-back guarantee, and include online publication and print in two bi-annual directories.

Best's Directory of Recommended Insurance Attorneys and Adjusters is distributed annually to insurance companies, self-insureds, claims managers, and corporate counsel and is also published online. The directory contains an Expert Services Section and a Consultants Section, sorted by discipline and geographical location. To advertise, an expert must have a minimum of five years' experience in his field and provide a list of clients that are law firms, insurance companies, or self-insureds. The A.M. Best Company will contact your references for an endorsement prior to publishing your listing.

The Casualty Adjuster's Guide contains the names and numbers of insurance companies, adjusters, appraisers, and claims associations, and is published for many geographic regions and online. The guide includes advertising from insurance services and also vendors such as experts. Most states have at least one guide and a few states have several guides for various areas of the state. Rates may differ slightly by region. The directories are mailed to every adjuster in their regions, and the names and addresses are updated annually. This is a significant point because of high industry turnover. If you advertise, you receive a copy of the guide, which you may want to use for contacting prospects.

The Claim Services Guide is a directory listing adjusters, appraisers, experts/consultants and repair and salvage companies, which is distributed annually to the insurance claims industry. *The Insurance Bar* is a directory of law firms whose practice is primarily insurance defense litigation. Both books, published by the Bar List Publishing Company, contain an Experts/Consultants section.

Networking

Contact chapters of insurance trade associations in the nearest metropolitan area. Ask to attend their meetings, and volunteer to speak to the group. Seminars and training sessions are usually well received. Limit the scope of your presentation and ensure that the audience is in tune with your topic. Make your presentation informational rather than trying to impress adjusters with your techno-speak. Have handouts with your contact information included, and linger afterwards to field questions and meet individuals.

At www.naiia.com, the National Association of Independent Insurance Adjusters lists the regional vice-presidents and their contact information. In addition, you can find information about insurance trade associations at the Web sites of some of the insurance publications previously mentioned.

You can also reach insurance prospects through personal networking. Erik Nelson, an architectural engineer with offices in Dallas and Houston, trades referral introductions to insurance people with related but non-competing experts such as roofing or foundation experts.

Remember to stay in touch with referral sources, along with clients and prospects, through means such as periodic mailings, described in the chapters on publicity and direct mail.

Referrals

With insurance prospects as well as all others, referrals are the most effective source of business. Once you have established a contact, be assertive in requesting referrals. Cultivate and nurture all referral sources.

THE INSURANCE COMPANY'S ATTORNEY

In addition to obtaining work directly from the insurance company you can contact law firms that you identify as representing insurance companies.

For personal injury defense work contact the insurance company and ask who handles their defense cases. It may be in-house counsel, or a public firm that handles cases for others as well. The larger insurance companies will have multiple outside counsel in various locales.

Medical malpractice defense is often handled by the larger law firms, which sometimes publicize the names of their most prestigious clients. You can decide which law firms to approach for this kind of work by determining which medical or hospital groups they represent. Legal publications occasionally publish lists of the largest or most successful law firms, with the lists also showing the law firms' primary clients. You can contact the dominant medical liability carriers to find out who represents them; you may be referred instead to their in-house counsel, but it never hurts to ask.

Law firms that represent insurance industry professionals are listed at www.insurancelawlist.com. These firms represent insurance companies and self-insured corporations located in the United States, Canada, and beyond. You can search by name, practice specialty, and/or location, and many of the law firms list their clients.

At the site, click on Corporate Counsel to find in-house lawyers for hundreds of major insurance companies. The contact information is not provided, as it is on the law firms, but the name of the attorney for each company is listed.

OPPORTUNITIES FOR INSURANCE WORK

Starting a forensic practice by conducting investigations or examinations for insurance claims offices can be a practical step. Insurers are more concerned with your ability to determine the facts involved with the claim than with your lack of courtroom experience.

Although most engineers and safety experts have a working knowledge of the insurance industry as a prospective client base, many medical doctors have previously worked only with the public. They may need to familiarize themselves with the insurance field as a source of work beyond patient care. In addition to doing medical record review and possibly testimony for attorneys, doctors can conduct Independent Medical Evaluations (IMEs) for insurance companies and attorneys. The majority of these cases do not go beyond the examination of the patient, the review of the medical records, and the doctor's written report. Sometimes, however, the doctor is required to testify in deposition or court as to his findings.

There is an industry of IME service companies that contract for work from insurance companies and attorneys and register doctors to provide the services. In addition to their greatest value in procuring the work, these agencies provide administrative services, which may include setting the appointment, billing and collecting, appointment cancellation compensation, and report transcription. The service may provide examination facilities, or the doctor may use his own office or a satellite office.

The service adds its fees to the doctor's rate, and provides corresponding value to the client by verifying the doctor's credentials before hiring him. Certain services may also review the doctor's report before sending it to the insurance company. Although the doctor might possibly be paid at a higher rate if he dealt directly with the insurance company, some of the insurance companies work only through IME services.

The recommendations stated in the chapter regarding referral agencies apply to IME service companies as well. Research the size of the service and its method of operation and marketing system, carefully review the contract regarding billing and collection, and require references. An additional caution to exercise when working with an IME agency: when sending your report through them, sign the report and keep a copy of your signed version to prevent any possibility of the report being altered. If you use their transcription service, do not sign blank reports to be filled in over your signature.

Another source of insurance work is legal nurse consultants. These medical/legal consultants work not only for attorneys, but also for insurers as independent case managers. Often they do an initial review of the case, perhaps a chronology and summary of treatment, and then hire physicians for medical review and possibly testimony and set up IME appointments. You can find nurse consultants in legal and insurance publications as well as online, as they advertise to solicit clients and recruit physicians.

Getting Paid for IMEs

The business practice recommendations in the chapter on billing and contracts apply to IME work as well as to expert witness work. The doctor should have a published fee schedule and policy statement. When possible, obtain pre-payment for at least the minimum time required. You should be allowed a reasonable amount of time to review records, examine the patient, and communicate a report. If adequate time is not allotted, the request may be for a rubber-stamp endorsement, rather than for an objective finding. Refuse to work for clients with such business practices. There are plenty of ethical insurance professionals.

COMMENTS REGARDING WORKING FOR INSURANCE COMPANIES

- "Insurance adjusters come and go; every six months there's a new guy." (Engineer)
- "Insurance companies pay very slowly." (Transportation Expert)
- "With insurance companies you will get paid." (Many Experts)
- "The attorney said that for him to be able to use me for insurance defense I should not publicize that I work for the plaintiff side as well." (Medical Doctor)
- "The key to getting paid more quickly by insurance people is to shape the invoice into smaller bites and deliver the billing with the work product. Once the billing and the work product become separated as to timing and proximity, the likelihood of the invoice getting handled becomes more remote." (Engineer)
- "An insurance adjuster wants to hear that 'there is no problem.'" (Safety Expert)
- "A seasoned adjuster wants an honest opinion – what reasonable loss am I facing?" (Medical Doctor)

CAUTION

Often the expert plays the role of confirming what the adjuster already knows. In this regard the independent expert's opinion is the one that counts. The expert's credibility, moreover, is always on the line, so delivering bad news is as critical as confirming good news. Nothing is more disastrous to an expert's reputation (never mind his personal integrity!) than becoming known for telling adjusters or attorneys only what they want to hear. If the client is looking for a "feel good" opinion, render only a verbal opinion and do not take the case.

CLOSING ARGUMENTS

You can do more than what is described in this book. *The Expert Witness Marketing Book* is a primer, to provide the expert witness with the information needed to perform basic marketing and to be a judicious purchaser of marketing services.

In addition to learning the mechanics, I hope you are convinced that:

1) Successful expert witness marketing includes the communication of your personal strengths and values, such as integrity, thoroughness, and the ability to communicate clearly. These attributes are most effectively demonstrated through networking and publicity. They are also reflected in the image you create with your materials, your appearance, and your advertising.

2) Communication is not something you choose to do. It is involuntary and continuous. Your choice is whether to take responsibility for it and make it contribute positively to your success.

Use the ideas from this book to express the right message to the right prospects using the right methods. This is the definition of marketing, and *you can do it!*

Rosalie Hamilton

RESOURCES

I apologize for the inadvertent omission of any particular item in this Resources section. Please send resource recommendations to Expert Communications, 140 Island Way, #288, Clearwater, Florida 33767.

Many of the books and other resources are available on my Web site, www.expertcommunications.com.

See "Resources/ECI Bookstore."

ATTORNEY BARS AND ASSOCIATIONS

In the interest of space, special interest bars are not listed.

National Bars and Associations

American Bar Association
750 North Lake Drive
Chicago, IL 60611
312-988-5000
Fax: 313-988-6281
www.abanet.org

Association of Trial Lawyers of America
1050 31st Street, N.W.
Washington, DC 20007-4499
202-965-3500
800-424-2725
Fax: 202-615-7313
www.atlanet.org

The Defense Research Institute, Inc.
150 North Michigan Avenue
Suite 300
Chicago, IL 60601
312-795-1101
Fax: 312-795-0747
www.dri.org

National Association of Criminal Defense Lawyers
1150 18th Street, N.W.
Suite 950
Washington, DC 20036
202-872-8600
Fax: 202-872-8690
www.criminaljustice.org

American Corporate Counsel Association
1025 Connecticut Avenue, N.W.
Suite 200
Washington, DC 20036-5425
202-293-4103
Fax: 202-293-4701
www.acca.com

State Bars and Associations

Alabama

Alabama State Bar
PO Box 671
Montgomery, AL 36101
334-269-1515
Fax: 334-261-6310
www.alabar.org

Alabama Trial Lawyers Association
770 Washington Avenue
Suite 170
Montgomery, AL 36104
334-262-4974
Fax: 334-262-1780
www.atla.org

Alabama Defense Lawyers Association
4269 Lomac Street
Montgomery, AL 36106
334-395-4455
Fax: 334-396-0211
www.adla.org

Alaska

Alaska State Bar Association
PO Box 100279
Anchorage, AK 99510-0279
907-272-7469
Fax: 907-272-2932
www.alaskabar.org

Alaska Academy of
Trial Lawyers
PO Box 102323
Anchorage, AK 99501
907-258-4040
Fax: 907-276-7185
www.aatl.org

Arizona

State Bar of Arizona
111 West Monroe Street
Suite 1800
Phoenix, AZ 85003-1742
602-252-4804
Fax: 602-271-4930
www.azbar.org

Arizona Trial Lawyers Association
1661 Camelback Road, Suite 204
Phoenix, AZ 85016
602-235-9356
Fax: 602-235-9331
www.aztla.org

Arkansas

Arkansas State Bar Association
Arkansas Bar Center
400 West Markham, Suite 401
Little Rock, AR 72201
501-375-4606
800-609-5668
Fax: 501-375-4901
www.arkbar.org

Arkansas Trial Lawyers
Association
PO Box 3468
Little Rock, AR 72203
501-376-2852
Fax: 501-372-0951
www.arktla.org

California

The State Bar of California
180 Howard Street
San Francisco, CA 94105-1639
415-538-2000
Fax: 415-538-2305
www.calbar.org

Consumer Attorneys of California
980 9th Street, Suite 200
Sacramento, CA 95814-2721
916-442-6902
Fax: 916-442-7734
www.caoc.com

Colorado

Colorado Bar Association
1900 Grant Street, Suite 900
Denver, CO 80203
303-860-1115
Fax: 303-894-0821
www.cobar.org

Colorado Trial Lawyers
Association
1888 Sherman Street, Suite 370
Denver, CO 80203
303-831-1192
Fax: 303-831-0111
www.ctla.org

Colorado Criminal Defense Bar
789 Sherman Street, Suite 660
Denver, CO 80203
303-758-2454
Fax: 303-830-1392
www.ccdb.org

Connecticut

Connecticut State Bar
PO Box 350
New Britain, CT 06050-0350
860-223-4400
Fax: 860-223-4488
www.ctbar.org

Connecticut Trial Lawyers Association
100 Wells Street, Suite 2H
Hartford, CT 06106
860-522-4325
Fax: 860-522-1027
www.ct-tla.org

Connecticut Criminal Defense Lawyers Association
C/o Lisa C. Cerverizzo,
Executive Director
PO Box 1776
Waterbury, CT 06721-1766
203-757-6354
Fax: 203-720-0388
www.ccdla.org

Delaware

Delaware State Bar Association
301 North Market Street
Wilmington, DE 19801
302-658-5279
800-292-7869 (*Kent & Sussex Counties*)
Fax: 302-658-5212
www.dsba.org

Delaware Trial Lawyers Association
715 King Street, Second Floor
Wilmington, DE 19801
302-421-2800
Fax: 302-421-2803
www.dtla.org

District of Columbia

The Bar Association of the District of Columbia (*Voluntary*)
1819 H Street, N.W., 12th Floor
Washington, DC 20006-3690
202-223-6600
Fax: 202-293-3388
www.badc.org

The District of Columbia Bar (*Mandatory*)
1250 H Street, N.W., 6th Floor
Washington, DC 20005-5937
202-737-4700
Fax: 202-626-3471
www.dcbar.org

Trial Lawyers Association of Metro Washington, DC
1100 Connecticut Avenue, N.W.
Suite 800
Washington, DC 20036
202-659-3532
Fax: 202-775-9040
www.tla-dc.org

District of Columbia Defense Lawyers Association
(*No executive office*)

Florida

Florida Bar Association
650 Appalachee Parkway
Tallahassee, FL 32399-2300
850-561-5600
Fax: 850-561-5826
www.flabar.org

Academy of Florida Trial Lawyers
218 South Monroe Street
Tallahassee, FL 32301
850-224-9403
Fax: 850-224-4254
www.aftl.org

Florida Defense Lawyers Association
2202 North West Shore Boulevard
Suite 200
Tampa, FL 33607
813-639-7585
Fax: 813-639-7586
www.fdla.org

Georgia

State Bar of Georgia
50 Hurt Plaza, Suite 1800
Atlanta, GA 30303
404-527-8700
800-334-6865
Fax: 404-527-8717
www.gabar.org

Georgia Trial Lawyers Association
1250 The Hurt Building
50 Hurt Plaza S.E.
Atlanta, GA 30303-2916
404-522-8487
800-843-4854 (*Outside Atlanta*)
Fax: 404-522-3705
www.gtla.org

Georgia Defense Lawyers Association
PO Box 246
Macon, GA 31202-0246
912-755-9813
www.gdla.org

Hawaii

Hawaii State Bar Association
1132 Bishop Street, Suite 906
Honolulu, HI 96813
808-537-1868
888-808-4722 (*Neighbor islands*)
Fax: 808-521-7936
www.hsba.org

Consumer Lawyers of Hawaii
1088 Bishop Street, Suite 1111
Honolulu, HI 96813
808-599-2769
Fax: 808-599-2859
www.clh.org

Idaho

Idaho State Bar
PO Box 895
Boise, ID 83701
208-334-4500
Fax: 208-334-4515
www.state.id.us/isb/

Idaho State Trial Lawyers Association
PO Box 1777
Boise, ID 83701
208-345-1890
Fax: 208-345-1894
www.itla.org

Illinois

Illinois State Bar Association
Illinois Bar Center
424 South Second Street
Springfield, IL 62701
217-525-1760
800-252-8908 (*In Illinois*)
Fax: 217-525-0712
www.illinoisbar.org

Illinois Trial Lawyers Association
PO Box 5000
Springfield, IL 62705
217-789-0755
800-252-8501
Fax: 217-789-0810
www.iltla.com

Illinois Association of Defense Trial Counsel
PO Box 7288
Springfield, IL 62791
217-636-7970
800-232-0169
Fax: 217-636-8812
www.iadtc.org

Indiana

Indiana State Bar Association
Indiana Bar Center
230 East Ohio Street, 4th Floor
Indianapolis, IN 46204-2119
317-639-5465
800-266-2581
Fax: 317-266-2588
www.state.in.us/isba

Indiana Trial Lawyers Association
150 West Market Street
ISTA Building
Indianapolis, IN 46204
317-634-8841
800-395-4852
Fax: 317-634-4898
www.i-t-l-a.org

Iowa

Iowa State Bar Association
521 East Locust, Suite 300
Des Moines, IA 50309-1939
515-243-3179
Fax: 515-243-2511
www.iowabar.org

Iowa Trial Lawyers Association
218 6th Avenue, Suite 526
Des Moines, IA 50309-4091
515-280-7366
800-373-4852
Fax: 515-280-3745
www.Iowatla.org

Kansas

Kansas Bar Association
PO Box 1037
Topeka, KS 66601-1037
785-234-5696
Fax: 785-234-3813
www.ksbar.org

Kansas Trial Lawyers Association
700 Southwest Jackson, Suite 706
Topeka, KS 66603-3758
785-232-7756
Fax: 785-232-7730

Kansas Association of Defense Counsel
300 Southwest Eighth Street
Third Floor
Topeka, KS 66603
785-232-9091
Fax: 785-233-2206
www.kadc.org

Kentucky

Kentucky Bar Association
514 West Main Street
Frankfurt, KY 40601-1883
502-564-3795
Fax: 502-564-3225
www.kybar.org

Kentucky Academy of
Trial Attorneys
10602 Timberwood Circle
Suite 8
Louisville, KY 40223
502-339-8890
Fax: 502-339-1780
www.kata.org

Kentucky Defense Counsel
5319 Rollingwood Trail
Louisville, KY 40214
502-380-1239
Fax: 502-380-0164

Louisiana

Louisiana State Bar Association
601 St. Charles Avenue
New Orleans, LA 70130-3404
504-566-1600
800-421-5722
Fax: 504-566-0930
www.lsba.org

Louisiana Trial Lawyers
Association
442 Europe Street
Baton Rouge, LA 70802
225-383-5554
800-354-6267
Fax: 225-387-1993
www.ltla.org

Louisiana Association of
Defense Lawyers
603 Europe Street
Baton Rouge, LA 70802
225-387-3261
Fax: 225-387-3262
www.lacdl.org

Maine

Maine State Bar Association
PO Box 788
Augusta, ME 04332-0788
207-622-7523
Fax: 207-623-0083
www.mainebar.org

Maine Trial Lawyers Association
PO Box 438
Augusta, ME 04332-0438
207-623-2661
Fax: 207-621-0118
www.mtla.org

Maine Association of
Criminal Defense Lawyers
One India Street
Portland, ME 04101
207-761-6938
Fax: 207-871-0164
http://home.gwi.net/~macdl/

Maryland

Maryland State Bar Association
Maryland Bar Center
520 West Fayette Street, Floor 2
Baltimore, MD 21201
410-685-7878
800-492-1964
Fax: 410-685-1016
www.msba.org

Maryland Trial Lawyers
Association
120 West Fayette Street, Suite 711
Baltimore, MD 21201
410-539-4336
Fax: 410-783-5981
www.mdtriallawyers.com

Maryland Criminal Defense
Attorneys' Association
720 Light Street
Baltimore, MD 21230
410-752-3318
Fax: 410-752-8295
www.mcdaa.org

Massachusetts

Massachusetts Bar Association
20 West Street
Boston, MA 02111-1218
617-338-0500
Fax: 617-542-3057
www.massbar.org

Massachusetts Academy of
Trial Attorneys
15 Broad Street, Suite 415
Boston, MA 02109
617-248-5858
Fax: 617-248-8701
www.massacademy.com

Massachusetts Association of
Criminal Defense Lawyers
PO Box 473
Newton, MA 02460
617-965-2271
Fax: 617-965-2215
www.macdl.com

Michigan

Michigan State Bar Association
306 Townsend Street
Lansing, MI 48933-2083
800-968-1442
Fax: 517-482-6248
www.michbar.org

Michigan Trial Lawyers
Association
504 South Creyts Road, Suite B
Lansing, MI 48917
517-321-3073
Fax: 517-321-4694
www.mtla.net

Michigan Defense Trial Counsel
700 North Washington Avenue
Lansing, MI 48906-5133
517-482-7538
Fax: 517-485-4129
www.mdtc.org

Minnesota

Minnesota State Bar Association
(*Voluntary*)
600 Nicollet Mall, Suite 380
Minneapolis, MN 55402
612-333-1183
800-882-6722
Fax: 612-333-4927
www.mnbar.org

Minnesota Trial Lawyers
Association
706 2nd Avenue South
140 Baker Building
Minneapolis, MN 55402
612-375-1707
800-898-6852
Fax: 612-334-3142
www.mntla.com

Minnesota Defense Lawyers
Association
600 Nicollet Mall, Suite 380-A
Minneapolis, MN 55401
612-338-2717
Fax: 612-333-4927
www.mdla.org

Mississippi

The Mississippi Bar
PO Box 2168
Jackson, MS 39225-2168
601-948-4471
Fax: 601-355-8635
www.msbar.org

Mississippi Trial Lawyers Association
PO Box 1992
Jackson, MS 39205
601-948-8631
Fax: 601-948-8633
www.mstla.com

Mississippi Defense Lawyers Association
PO Box 5605
Brandon, MS 39047
601-992-8645
Fax: 601-992-2852
www.msdefenselaw.org

Missouri

Missouri State Bar Association
PO Box 119
Jefferson City, MO 65102
573-635-4128
Fax: 573-635-2811
www.mobar.org

Missouri Association of Trial Attorneys
PO Box 1792
Jefferson City, MO 65102-1792
573-635-5215
Fax: 573-634-6282
www.matanet.org

Missouri Association of Criminal Defense Lawyers
PO Box 1543
Jefferson City, MO 65102
573-636-2822
Fax: 573-636-9749
www.macdl.net

Montana

State Bar of Montana
PO Box 577
Helena, MT 59624
406-442-7660
Fax: 406-442-7763
www.montanabar.org

Montana Trial Lawyers Association
PO Box 838
Helena, MT 59624
406-443-3124
Fax: 406-449-6943
www.monttla.com

Montana Defense Trial Lawyers Association
36 South Last Chance Gulch
Suite A
Helena, MT 59601
406-443-1160
Fax: 406-443-4614
www.mdtl.net

Nebraska

Nebraska State Bar Association
PO Box 81809
Lincoln, NE 68501
402-475-7091
Fax: 402-475-7098
www.nebar.com

Nebraska Association of Trial Attorneys
941 "O" Street, Suite 203
Lincoln, NE 68508
402-435-5526
Fax: 402-435-5547
www.nebraskatrial.com

Nevada

State Bar of Nevada
600 East Charleston Boulevard
Las Vegas, NV 89104
702-382-2200
Fax: 702-385-2878
www.nvbar.org

Nevada Trial Lawyers Association
406 North Nevada Street
Carson City, NV 89703-4624
775-883-3577
Fax: 775-883-5372
www.ntla.org

New Hampshire

New Hampshire State Bar Association
112 Pleasant Street
Concord, NH 03301
603-224-6942
Fax: 603-224-2910
www.nhbar.org

New Hampshire Trial Lawyers Association
PO Box 447
Concord, NH 03302-0447
603-224-7077
Fax: 603-224-3256
www.nhtla.org

New Jersey

New Jersey State Bar Association
New Jersey Law Center
One Constitution Square
New Brunswick, NJ 08901-1520
732-249-5000
Fax: 732-249-2815
www.njsba.com

Association of Trial Lawyers of America – New Jersey
150 West State Street, Capitol View
Trenton, NJ 08608
609-396-0096
Fax: 609-396-2463
www.atlanj.org

New Jersey Defense Association
PO Box 463
Linwood, NJ 08221
609-927-1180
Fax: 609-927-4540
www.njdefenseassoc.com

New Mexico

State Bar of New Mexico
PO Box 25883
Albuquerque, NM 87125
505-797-6000
Fax: 505-828-3765
www.nmbar.org

New Mexico Trial Lawyers Association
PO Box 301
Albuquerque, NM 87103-0301
505-243-6003
Fax: 505-243-6099
www.nmtla.org

**New Mexico Criminal
Defense Lawyers Association**
PO Box 8324
Santa Fe, NM 87504-8180
505-986-9536

New York

New York State Bar Association
One Elk Street
Albany, NY 12207
518-463-3200
Fax: 518-487-5564
www.nysba.org

**New York State Trial Lawyers
Association**
132 Nassau Street, 2nd Floor
New York, NY 10038
212-349-5890
Fax: 212-608-2310
www.nystla.org

**New York State
Defenders Association**
194 Washington Avenue
Suite 500
Albany, NY 12210
518-465-3524
Fax: 518-465-3249
www.nysda.org

**New York State Association of
Criminal Defense Lawyers**
475 Park Avenue S., Suite 3300
New York, NY 10016
212-532-4434
Fax: 212-532-4668
www.nysacdl.org

North Carolina

**North Carolina Bar Association
(*Voluntary*)**
PO Box 3688
Cary, NC 27519
919-677-0561
Fax: 919-677-0761
www.barlinc.org

**North Carolina State Bar
(*Mandatory*)**
PO Box 25908
Raleigh, NC 27611
919-828-4620
Fax: 919-821-9168
www.ncbar.com

**North Carolina Academy of
Trial Lawyers**
PO Box 10918
Raleigh, NC 27605-0918
919-832-1413
800-688-1413
Fax: 919-832-6361
www.ncatl.org

**North Carolina Association of
Defense Attorneys**
PO Box 4830
Cary, NC 27519-4830
919-677-0561
800-233-2858
Fax: 919-677-0761
www.ncada.org

North Dakota

**State Bar Association of
North Dakota**
515½ East Broadway, Suite 101
Bismarck, ND 58501
701-225-1404
800-472-2085 (*In state*)
Fax: 701-224-1621
www.sband.org

North Dakota Trial
Lawyers Association
PO Box 365
Mandan, ND 58554
701-663-3916
Fax: 701-663-3917
www.ndtla.com

Ohio

Ohio State Bar Association
PO Box 16562
Columbus, OH 43216-6562
614-487-2050
800-282-6556
Fax: 614-487-1008
www.ohiobar.org

Ohio Academy of Trial Lawyers
395 East Broad Street
Suite 200
Columbus, OH 43215
614-341-6800
Fax: 614-341-6810
www.oatlaw.org

**Ohio Association of
Criminal Defense Lawyers**
PO Box 545
Grove City, OH 43123
614-542-5720
800-443-2626
Fax: 614-542-5756
www.oacdl.org

Oklahoma

Oklahoma Bar Association
PO Box 53036
Oklahoma City, OK 73152-3036
405-416-7000
Fax: 405-416-7001
www.okbar.org

**Oklahoma Trial Lawyers
Association**
323 Northeast 27th Street
Oklahoma City, OK 73105
405-525-8044
Fax: 405-528-2431
www.otla.org

Oregon

Oregon State Bar
PO Box 1689
Lake Oswego, OR 97035
503-620-0222
Fax: 503-684-1366
www.osbar.org

Oregon Trial Lawyers Association
1020 Southwest Taylor
Suite 400
Portland, OR 97205
503-223-5587
Fax: 503-223-4101
www.oregontriallawyers.org

**Oregon Criminal Defense
Lawyers Association**
44 West Broadway, Suite 403
Eugene, OR 97401
541-686-8716
Fax: 541-686-2319
www.ocdla.org

Pennsylvania

**Pennsylvania State
Bar Association**
PO Box 186
Harrisburg, PA 17108-0186
717-238-6715
Fax: 717-238-1204
www.pabar.org

Pennsylvania Trial Lawyers
Association
121 South Broad Street
Suite 800
Philadelphia, PA 19107-4594
215-546-6451
Fax: 215-546-5430
www.patla.org

Pennsylvania Defense Institute
133 State Street
Harrisburg, PA 17101
717-238-7806
800-734-0737
Fax: 717-238-2766
www.padefense.org

Rhode Island

Rhode Island State Bar
Association
115 Cedar Street
Providence, RI 02903
401-421-5740
Fax: 401-421-2703
www.ribar.com

Rhode Island Trial
Lawyers Association
One Park Row
Providence, RI 02903
401-273-8820
Fax: 401-521-3350

Rhode Island Association of
Criminal Defense Lawyers
9 Pinehurst Avenue
Providence, RI 02906
401-222-1526
Fax: 401-222-3289
www.firms.findlaw.com/riacdl/

South Carolina

South Carolina Bar Association
PO Box 608
Columbia, SC 29202
803-799-6653
Fax: 803-799-4118
www.scbar.org

South Carolina Trial
Lawyers Association
PO Box 11557
Columbia, SC 29211
803-799-5097
Fax: 803-799-1041
www.sctla.org

South Carolina Defense
Trial Attorneys
3008 Millwood Avenue
Columbia, SC 29205
803-252-5646
800-445-8629
Fax: 803-765-0860
www.scdtaa.com

South Dakota

South Dakota State
Bar Association
222 East Capitol Avenue
Pierre, SD 57501
605-224-7554
800-952-2333
Fax: 605-224-0282
www.sdbar.org

South Dakota Trial
Lawyers Association
PO Box 1154
Pierre, SD 57501-1154
605-224-9292
Fax: 605-945-1204
www.sdtla.com

South Dakota Defense
Lawyers Association
www.rapidnet.com/sddla

Tennessee

Tennessee Bar Association
221 4th Avenue N.
Suite 400
Nashville, TN 37219
615-383-7421
Fax: 615-297-8058
www.tba.org

Tennessee Trial Lawyers
Association
1903 Division Street
Nashville, TN 37203
615-329-3000
Fax: 615-329-8131
www.ttla.org

Tennessee Association of
Criminal Defense Lawyers
207 Third Avenue N.
Second Floor, Suite 510
Nashville, TN 37201-1610
615-726-1225
Fax: 615-726-5859
www.racdl.org/tacdl/

Texas

Texas Bar Association
PO Box 12487
Austin, TX 78711-2487
512-463-1463
800-204-2222
Fax: 512-463-1475
www.texasbar.com

Texas Trial Lawyers Association
PO Box 788
Austin, TX 78767
512-476-3852
Fax: 512-473-2411
www.ttla.com

Texas Association of
Defense Counsel
400 West 15th Street, Suite 315
Austin, TX 78701
512-476-5225
Fax: 512-476-5384
www.tadc.org

Texas Criminal Defense
Lawyers Association
600 West 13th Street
Austin, TX 78701
512-478-2514
Fax: 512-469-9107
www.tcdla.com

Utah

Utah State Bar
645 South 200 E., Suite 310
Salt Lake City, UT 84111-3834
801-531-9077
Fax: 801-531-0660
www.utahbar.org

Utah Trial Lawyers Association
645 South 200 E., Suite 103
Salt Lake City, UT 84111
801-531-7514
Fax: 801-531-1207
www.utla.org

Utah Association of
Criminal Defense Lawyers
PO Box 510846
Salt Lake City, UT 84151
801-524-4010
Fax: 801-524-4060
www.uacdl.org

Vermont

Vermont State Bar Association
PO Box 100
Montpelier, VT 05601-0100
802-223-2020
Fax: 802-223-1573
www.vtbar.org

Vermont Trial Lawyers Association
100 State Street, Suite 332
Montpelier, VT 05602
802-223-0501
Fax: 802-223-4880
www.vtla.org

Virginia

Virginia State Bar Association (*Mandatory*)
707 East Main Street, Suite 1500
Richmond, VA 23219-2800
804-775-0500
Fax: 804-775-0501
www.vsb.org

Virginia Bar Association (*Voluntary*)
7th & Franklin Building
701 East Franklin Street
Suite 1120
Richmond, VA 23219
804-644-0041
Fax: 804-644-0052
www.vba.org

Virginia Trial Lawyers Association
700 East Main Street, Suite 1510
Richmond, VA 23219
804-343-1143
800-267-8852
Fax: 804-343-7124
www.vtla.com

Virginia Association of Defense Attorneys
707 East Main Street, Suite 1605
Richmond, VA 23219
804-649-1002
Fax: 804-649-1004
www.vada.org

Washington

Washington State Bar Association
2101 4th Avenue, Suite 400
Seattle, WA 98121-2330
206-443-9722
Fax: 206-727-8320
www.wsba.org

Washington State Trial Lawyers Association
1809 7th Avenue, Suite 1500
Seattle, WA 98101-1328
209-464-1011
Fax: 206-464-0703
www.wstla.org

Washington Defense Trial Lawyers Association
1601 5th Avenue, Suite 2400
Seattle, WA 98101
206-521-6559
Fax: 206-521-6501
www.wdtl.org

West Virginia

West Virginia State Bar Association (*Mandatory*)
2006 Kanawha Boulevard East
Charleston, WV 25311-2204
304-558-2456
Fax: 304-558-2467
www.wvbar.org

West Virginia Bar Association
(*Voluntary*)
PO Box 3956
Charleston, WV 25339
304-346-5688
Fax: 304-346-5689

West Virginia Trial
Lawyers Association
PO Box 3968
Charleston, WV 25339
304-344-0692
Fax: 304-343-7926
www.wvtla.org

Defense Trial Counsel of
West Virginia
www.dtcwv.org

Wisconsin

The State Bar of Wisconsin
PO Box 7158
Madison, WI 53707-7158
608-257-3838
800-728-7788
Fax: 608-257-5502
www.wisbar.org

Wisconsin Academy of
Trial Lawyers
44 East Mifflin Street, Suite 103
Madison, WI 53703-2897
608-257-5741
Fax: 608-255-9285
www.watl.org

Civil Trial Counsel of Wisconsin
1123 North Water Street
Milwaukee, WI 53202
414-276-1881
Fax: 414-276-7704
www.ctcw.org

Wisconsin Association of
Criminal Defense Lawyers
PO Box 2116
Madison, WI 53701-2116
608-255-9822
Fax: 608-255-6711
www.wacdl.com

Wyoming

Wyoming State Bar Association
PO Box 109
Cheyenne, WY 82003-0109
307-632-9061
Fax: 307-632-3737
www.wyomingbar.org

Wyoming Trial Lawyers
Association
2111 Warren Avenue
Cheyenne, WY 82001
307-635-0820
Fax: 307-634-5331
www.wytla.org

Defense Lawyers Association
of Wyoming
www.dlaw-wyoming.com

BOOKS

Expert Witness Book Publishing/Marketing Companies

Expert Communications
140 Island Way, #288
Clearwater, FL 33767
727-467-0700
866-467-0801
Fax: 727-467-0800
www.expertcommunications.com

LRP Publications
PO Box 980
Horsham, PA 19044
215-784-0860
800-341-7874
Fax: 215-784-9639
www.lrp.com

National Forensic Center
17 Temple Terrace
Lawrenceville, NJ 08648
609-883-0550
800-526-5177
Fax: 609-883-7622
www.expertindex.com

SEAK, Inc.
PO Box 729
Falmouth, MA 02541
505-457-1111
Fax: 508-540-8304
www.seak.com

Expert Witness Books

This list is a sample of the best "how-to" expert witness books. For a more comprehensive list, refer to the resources section of *The Expert Witness Handbook: Tips and Techniques for the Litigation Consultant,* by Dan Poynter.

The Art and Science of Expert Witnessing
Olen R. Brown, PH.D.
Cypress Publishing Group, Inc.
11835 Roe, #187
Leawood, KS 66211
800-284-7328
Fax: 913-498-1524
www.cypresspublishing.com

The Comprehensive Forensic Services Manual
Steven Babitsky, J.D.,
James J. Mangraviti, Jr., J.D., &
Christopher J. Todd, J.D.
SEAK, Inc.
PO Box 729
Falmouth, MA 02541
505-457-1111
Fax: 508-540-8304
www.seak.com

The Consultant's Guide to
Litigation Services: How to be
an Expert Witness
Thomas H. Veitch, J.D.
John Wiley & Sons, Inc.
(*Available through bookstores*)

Courtroom Guide for
Non-Lawyers
Benjamin J. Cantor
Xlibris Corporation
888-795-4274
www.xlibris.com

The Expert Witness Handbook:
Tips and Techniques for the
Litigation Consultant
Dan Poynter
Para Publishing
PO Box 8206-978
Santa Barbara, CA 93118-8206
805-968-7277
800-727-2782
Fax: 805-968-1379
www.parapub.com

The Forensic Expert's Guide
to Litigation: The Anatomy
of a Lawsuit
Marc A. Rabinoff, ED.D. &
Stephen P. Holmes, ESQ.
LRP Publications
PO Box 980
Horsham, PA 19044-0980
215-784-0860
800-341-7874
Fax: 215-784-9639
www.lrp.com

The Guide to Experts' Fees
National Forensic Center
17 Temple Terrace
Lawrenceville, NJ 08648
609-883-0550
800-526-5177
Fax: 609-883-7622
www.expertindex.com

Succeeding as an Expert Witness:
Increasing Your Impact and
Income
Harold A. Feder, ESQ.
Tageh Press
PO Box 401
Glenwood Springs, CO 81602-0401
800-468-2434
www.montrose.net/tageh

CONFERENCES

All-Disciplines Forensic Conferences

National Forensic Center
17 Temple Terrace
Lawrenceville, NJ 08448
609-883-0550
800-526-5177
Fax: 609-883-7622
www.expertindex.com

SEAK, Inc.
PO Box 729
Falmouth, MA 02541
508-457-1111
Fax: 508-540-8304
www.seak.com

Other Forensic Conferences

**American Academy of
Forensic Sciences**
PO Box 669
Colorado Springs, CO 80901-0669
719-636-1100
Fax: 719-636-1993
www.aafs.org

**American College of
Forensic Examiners**
2750 Sunshine Street
Springfield, MO 65804
417-881-3818
Fax: 417-881-4702
www.acfe.com

**American College of
Legal Medicine**
611 East Wells Street
Milwaukee, WI 53202
414-276-1881
800-433-9137
Fax: 414-276-3349
www.aclm.org

Professional Association Forensic Conferences

Contact your national and state professional associations for litigation related conferences.

INTERNET EXPERT WITNESS DIRECTORIES

This list does not constitute endorsement of any particular site.

Referral services that also have Internet sites are listed in "Resources/Referral Services."

Internet expert witness directories that charge the user to find an expert witness or are involved in the financial arrangements between attorney and expert witness are listed in "Resources/Referral Services."

General Internet Expert Witness Directories

www.alllaw.com

www.bestlawyers.com

www.ca-experts.com

www.ewitness.com

www.expertlaw.com

www.expertpages.com

www.experts.com

www.expertwitness.com

www.findlaw.com

www.hg.org

www.jurispro.com

www.jurissolutions.com

www.law.com

www.lawfirmpro.com

www.lawinfo.com

www.lawsonline.com

www.morelaw.com

www.romingerlegal.com

www.theattorneystore.com

www.witness.net

Internet Expert Witness Directories that are Also Print Directories

See "Resources/Print Expert Witness Directories" for contact information.

www.abve.net
American Board of Vocational Experts Membership Directory

www.ambest.com
Best Directory of Recommended Insurance Attorneys & Adjusters

www.astm.org
ASTM Directory of Scientific & Technical Consultants & Expert Witnesses

www.barlist.com
The Claim Services Guide
The Insurance Guide

www.cagworld.com
Casualty Adjuster Guide

www.claims.com
The National Directory of Expert Witnesses

www.expert4law.org
Southern California Directory of Experts & Consultants

www.expertindex.com
National Forensic Center Forensic Services Directory

www.martindale.com
The Martindale-Hubbell® Buyer's Guide

www.nljexperts.com
The National Law Journal Expert Witnesses & Consultants Directories

www.seak.com
National Directory of Independent Medical Examiners™

National Directory of Medical Experts™

www.sfbar.org
Northern California Register of Experts and Consultants

Internet Expert Witness Directory that is a Reproduction of Newspaper Ads

www.lawyersweeklyexperts.com
Lawyers Weekly Newspapers

Internet Sites for Professional Membership Directories

See "Resources/Print Expert Witness Directories/Professional Association Membership Directories."

Expert (*Not Expert Witness*) Directories

Examples:

www.expertclick.com
The Yearbook of Experts, Authorities & Spokespersons

www.findexperts.com

EXPERT WITNESS JOURNALS AND NEWSLETTERS

These publications cover a large number of disciplines. Some are free and others charge for a subscription. Also check Internet expert witness directory sites for informative newsletters.

The Forensic Examiner
American College of
Forensic Examiners
2750 Sunshine Street
Springfield, MO 65804
417-881-3818
Fax: 417-881-4702
www.acfe.com

Journal of Forensic Sciences
American Academy of
Forensic Sciences
PO Box 669
Colorado Springs, CO 80901-0669
719-636-1100
Fax: 719-636-1993
www.aafs.org

Scientific Sleuthing Review
C/o Prof. James E. Starrs
National Law School
The George Washington University
Washington, DC 20052
202-994-6770
Fax: 202-994-9446

The Testifying Expert
LRP Publications
PO Box 980
Horsham, PA 19044
215-784-0860
800-341-7874
Fax: 215-784-9639
www.lrp.com

MISCELLANEOUS

Courtroom Communication Training

David M. Benjamin, PH.D.
77 Florence Street, Suite 107
Chestnut Hill, MA 02467
617-969-1393
Fax: 617-969-4285

Insurance

James A. Misselwitz
Evans Conger Broussard & McCrea
One Bala Plaza, Suite 640
Bala Cynwd, PA 19004-1401
610-668-7100
888-313-3226
Fax: 610-667-2208
www.ecbm.com

Legal Markets Convention & Trade Show Calendar

Nathan's Marketing & Trade Show Report
Nathan's Legal Markets
650 Third Avenue, Suite 1650
Minneapolis, MN 55402
952-935-9793
Fax: 952-935-9711
www.nathanslegalmarkets.com

PERIODICALS

Attorney Organization Publications

See "Resources/Attorney Bars and Associations" for contact information.

National

ABA Journal
American Bar Association

ACCA Docket
American Corporate Counsel Association

The Champion
National Association of Criminal Defense Lawyers

For the Defense
(*Does not accept advertising*)
The Defense Research Institute, Inc.

Trial
Association of Trial Lawyers of America

State, Local, and Regional

Contact the following to determine whether they publish magazines for their members and whether they accept advertising from and/or articles written by expert witnesses. See "Resources/Attorney Bars and Associations" for contact information.

- State bar association
- State association for plaintiff attorneys
- State association for defense attorneys
- State association for criminal defense attorneys
- Local or regional bar association

Commercial Publications

AMERICAN LAWYER MEDIA, INC.
www.americanlawyermedia.com

National Publications

The American Lawyer
345 Park Avenue S.
New York, NY 10010
212-779-9200
800-888-8300
Fax: 212-481-8255
www.americanlawyer.com

Corporate Counsel
(See *The American Lawyer*)

The National Law Journal
105 Madison Avenue, 8th Floor
New York, NY 10016
212-313-9180
800-537-2128
Fax: 212-585-8441
www.nlj.com

Regional Publications

Broward Daily Business Review
633 West Andrews Avenue
Fort Lauderdale, FL 33301
954-468-2600
Fax: 954-944-9451

The Connecticut Law Tribune
(See *Law Tribune* Newspapers)

Daily Report
190 Pryor Street, S.W.
Atlanta, GA 30303
404-521-1227
Fax: 404-523-5924
www.fcdr.com

Delaware Law Weekly
(See *Pennsylvania Law Weekly*)

Florida Lawyer
(See *Miami Daily Business Review*)

Law Tribune Newspapers
201 Ann Street, 4th Floor
Hartford, CT 06103
860-527-7900
Fax: 860-527-7433

The Legal Intelligencer
(See *Pennsylvania Law Weekly*)

Legal Times
1730 M Street, N.W., Suite 802
Washington, DC 20036
202-457-0686
Fax: 202-785-4539

Miami Daily Business Review
One Southeast Third Avenue
Suite 900
Miami, FL 33131
305-377-3721
Fax: 305-374-8474

New Jersey Law Journal
PO Box 20081
Newark, NJ 07101
973-642-0075
Fax: 973-642-0920

New York Law Journal
345 Park Avenue S.
New York, NY 10010
212-779-9200
800-888-8300
Fax: 212-481-8074

Palm Beach Daily Business Review
100 South Dixie Highway
West Palm Beach, FL 33401
561-820-2060
Fax: 561-820-2077

Pennsylvania Law Weekly
1617 J.F.K. Boulevard, Suite 1750
Philadelphia, PA 19103
215-557-2393
800-722-7670
Fax: 215-557-2301
www.law.com/pennsylvania

The Recorder
Ten United Nations Plaza
Third Floor
San Francisco, CA 94102
415-749-5400
Fax: 415-749-5430
www.therecorder.com

Texas Lawyer
900 Jackson Street, Suite 500
Dallas, TX 75202
214-744-7700
800-456-5484
Fax: 214-741-2325

*The Western Massachusetts
Law Tribune*
225 Friend Street
Boston, MA 02114-1812
866-529-8742
Fax: 617-725-0092

DAILY JOURNAL CORPORATION
www.dailyjournal.com

Regional Publications

Arizona Journal
1505 North Central Avenue
Suite 200
Phoenix, AZ 85004
602-417-9900
Fax: 602-417-9910

California Lawyer
1145 Market Street, 8th Floor
San Francisco, CA 94103
415-252-0500
Fax: 415-252-0288

Colorado Journal
Manville Plaza, Suite 2710
717 Seventeenth Street
Denver, CO 80202
303-222-3200
Fax: 303-292-5821

Los Angeles Daily Journal
915 East First Street
Los Angeles, CA 90012
213-229-5300
Fax: 213-680-3682

Nevada Journal
333 South Third Street
Las Vegas, NV 89101
702-385-9575
Fax: 213-680-3682

San Francisco Daily Journal
(See *California Lawyer*)

Washington Journal
(See *Los Angeles Daily Journal*)

LAWYERS WEEKLY, INC.
www.lawyersweekly.com

National Publication

Lawyers Weekly USA
41 West Street
Boston, MA 02111-1233
617-451-7300
800-444-5297
Fax: 617-451-0249
www.lawyersweekly.com

Regional Publications

Massachusetts Lawyers Weekly
41 West Street
Boston, MA 02111-1233
617-451-7300
800-444-5297
Fax: 617-451-7326
www.masslaw.com

Michigan Lawyers Weekly
39500 Orchard Hill Place Drive
Suite 155
Lansing, MI 48375
248-596-2700
800-678-5297
Fax: 517-596-2720
www.milawyersweekly.com

Missouri Lawyers Weekly
515 Olive Street, Suite 1606
St. Louis, MO 63101
314-621-8500
800-635-5297
Fax: 314-621-1913
www.molawyersweekly.com

North Carolina Lawyers Weekly
107 Fayetteville Street Mall
Raleigh, NC 27601
919-829-9333
800-876-5297
Fax: 919-828-5667
www.nclawyersweekly.com

Ohio Lawyers Weekly
11470 Euclid Avenue, Suite 513
Cleveland, OH 44106-9926
617-218-8312
800-935-5297
Fax: 617-451-7329
www.ohiolawyersweekly.com

Rhode Island Lawyers Weekly
(See *Massachusetts
Lawyers Weekly*)
www.rilawyersweekly.com

South Carolina Lawyers Weekly
(See *North Carolina
Lawyers Weekly*)
www.sclawyersweekly.com

Virginia Lawyers Weekly
801 East Main Street, Suite 201
Richmond, VA 23219
804-783-0770
800-456-5297
Fax: 804-343-1932
www.virginialaw.com

PRINT EXPERT
WITNESS DIRECTORIES

Comprehensive Expert
Witness Directories

Forensic Services Directory
National Forensic Center
PO Box 3161
Princeton, NJ 08543
609-883-0550
800-526-5177
Fax: 609-883-7622
www.expertindex.com

Lemark Comprehensive
Guides to Expert Witnesses
and Legal Professionals
Lemark Regional Editions—
Southern Edition
Western Edition
North Central Edition
Northeastern Edition
1003 Central Avenue
PO Box 1052
Fort Dodge, IA 50501
800-718-2288
Fax: 515-573-8031
www.lemarkregionals.com

Martindale-Hubbell®
Buyer's Guide
Martindale-Hubbell®
121 Chanlon Road
New Providence, NJ 07974
800-526-4902
www.martindale.com

The National Directory
of Expert Witnesses
Claims Providers of America
PO Box 395
Esparto, CA 95627
800-735-6660
Fax: 916-796-3631
www.claims.com

The National Law Journal
(formerly *American Lawyer*
Media) *Directories of Expert*
Witnesses & Consultants
Mid-Atlantic
Midwestern
National Medical
New England
New Jersey
New York
Southeastern
Southwestern
Western (formerly
   Legal Expert Pages)

Northern California Register of
Experts and Consultants
Bar Association of San Francisco
465 Market Square, Suite 1100
San Francisco, CA 94104-1826
415-781-8922
Fax: 415-782-8994
www.sfbar.org

Southern California Directory
of Experts & Consultants
Los Angeles County
Bar Association
PO Box 55020
Los Angeles, CA 90055
213-896-6470
Fax: 213-613-1909
www.expert4law.org

Discipline Specific Expert Witness Directories

American Board of Forensic Psychology Directory of Diplomates
American Academy of
Forensic Psychology
638 Poplar Court
Pittsburgh, PA 15238
412-828-9685
Fax: 412-826-8279
www.abfp.com

American Board of Vocational Experts Membership Directory
3540 Soquel Avenue, Suite A
Santa Cruz, CA 95062
831-464-4890
Fax: 831-576-1417
www.abve.net

ASTM Directory of Scientific & Technical Consultants & Expert Witnesses
ASTM International
100 Barr Harbor Drive, Box C700
West Conshohocken, PA 19428-2959
610-832-9611
Fax: 610-832-9635
www.astm.org

NAFE Directory
National Academy of
Forensic Engineers
174 Brady Avenue
Hawthorne, NY 10532
866-623-3674
Fax: 877-741-0633
www.nafe.org

SEAK National Directory of Independent Medical Examiners™
SEAK, Inc.
PO Box 729
Falmouth, MA 02541
508-548-7023
Fax: 508-540-8304
www.imenet.com

SEAK National Directory of Medical Experts™
SEAK, Inc.
PO Box 729
Falmouth, MA 02541
508-548-7023
Fax: 508-540-8304
www.seakmedexperts.com

Expert (*Not Expert Witness*) Directories

Example:

The Yearbook of Experts, Authorities & Spokespersons
Broadcast Interview Source
2233 Wisconsin Avenue, N.W.
Washington, DC 20007
202-333-4904
Fax: 202-342-5411
www.expertclick.com

Insurance Directories

Best's Directory of Recommended Insurance Attorneys and Adjusters
A.M. Best Company
Ambest Road
Oldwick, NJ 08858
908-439-2200
800-439-2200
Fax: 908-439-2688
www.ambest.com

Casualty Adjuster's Guide (*CAG*)
www.cagworld.com

The Claim Service Guide
Bar List Publishing Company
PO Box 40580
Cleveland, OH 44140-0580
800-533-2500
Fax: 440-835-3636
www.barlist.com

The Insurance Bar
Bar List Publishing Company

Professional Association Membership Directories

Association membership lists are sometimes used by attorneys to locate expert witnesses.

American Academy of Forensic Sciences Membership Directory
PO Box 669
Colorado Springs, CO 80901-0669
719-636-1100
Fax: 719-636-1993
www.aafs.org

American College of Forensic Examiners Membership Directory
2750 East Sunshine Street
Springfield, MO 65804-2047
417-881-3818
Fax: 417-881-4702
www.acfe.com

American Council of Engineering Companies Membership Directory
1015 15th Street, N.W., Suite 802
Washington, DC 20005
202-347-7474
Fax: 202-898-0068
www.acec.org

American Polygraph Association
Membership Directory
PO Box 8037
Chattanooga, TN 37414-0037
800-272-8037
Fax: 423-894-5435
www.polygraph.org

ASFE Membership Directory
(Formerly *ASFE: Professional Firms Practicing in the Geosciences*)
(Formerly Association of Soil & Foundation Engineers)
8811 Colesville Road, Suite G106
Silver Spring, MD 20910
301-565-2733
Fax: 301-589-2017
www.asfe.org

Directory of Professional Appraisers
American Society of Appraisers
555 Herndon Parkway, Suite 125
Herndon, VA 20170
703-478-2228
800-272-8258
Fax: 703-742-8471
www.appraisers.org

PATCA Directory of Consultants
Professional & Technical Consultants Association
1060 North Fourth Street
San Jose, CA 95112
408-971-5902
800-747-2822
Fax: 408-999-0344
www.patca.org

REFERRAL SERVICES

Attorney Associations

Availability and requirements of referral databases vary from association to association. Attorneys might be required to input listings. Contact individual associations for details. See "Resources/Attorney Bars and Associations" for contact information.

National Attorney Associations

American Bar Association
(No referral service)

American Corporate Counsel Association
(No referral service)

Association of Trial Lawyers of America

The Defense Research Institute, Inc.

National Association of Criminal Defense Lawyers

State Attorney Associations

Examples:

Texas Trial Lawyers Association
(No referral service)

Texas Association of Defense Counsel

Texas Criminal Defense Lawyers Association
(No referral service)

Commercial Referral Services

There are numerous expert witness referral services, especially medical related. I apologize for any exclusion; a complete list would comprise a book by itself. Certain other, non-medical services are also industry specific, rather than serving all disciplines.

A.C.E. (Analytical Consulting Experts) Services
PO Box 90938
Houston, TX 77290-0938
281-893-6075
800-347-3029
Fax: 281-350-1407

American Medical Forensics Specialists, Inc.
2991 Shattuck Avenue, Suite 302
Berkeley, CA 94705-1872
510-549-1693
800-275-8903
Fax: 510-486-1255
www.amfs.com

Benchmark Administrative Services Company
601 University Avenue, Suite 225
Sacramento, CA 95825
800-458-1261
Fax: 888-458-1261
www.benchmarkadmin.com

CECON Consulting Group
Science and Engineering Consulting Network
Tower Office Park, Newport
242 North James Street
Wilmington, DE 19804-3168
301-994-8000
888-263-8000
Fax: 302-994-8837
www.cecon.com

The Chatham Group
101 First Street, Suite 477
Los Altos, CA 94022
650-948-1243
Fax: 650-949-0534
www.chathamlaw.com

**Consolidated Consultants
Company**
739 Twin Oaks Avenue
Chula Vista, CA 91910
619-422-5559
800-683-9847
Fax: 619-422-8101
www.freereferral.com

DJS Associates, Inc.
1603 Old York Road
Abington, PA 19001
215-659-2010
800-332-6273
Fax: 215-659-7156
www.forensicdjs.com

Expert Resources, Inc.
4700 North Prospect Road
Suite 1B
Peoria Heights, IL 61614-6428
309-688-4857
800-383-4857
Fax: 888-815-2778
www.expertresources.com

Forensic Expert Advisors, Inc.
3305 South Woodland Place
Santa Ana, CA 92707
714-754-4332
800-584-8178
Fax: 714-754-7432
www.forensic-experts.com

JD.MD,™ Inc.
PO Box 11733
Atlanta, GA 30355-1733
404-846-9115
800-225-5363
Fax: 404-846-9185
www.jdmd.com

Juris Solutions, Inc.
550 Old Country Road, Suite 407
Hicksville, NY 11801
516-935-8747
877-835-8750
Fax: 516-935-8748

Maritime & Aviation Consultants
3790 El Camino Real, Suite 207
Palo Alto, CA 94306-3314
877-574-1120
Fax: 650-745-2413
www.mac-experts.com

Medco Associates, Inc.
1603 Olympus Drive
Austin, TX 78733
512-263-0322
800-341-6461
Fax: 512-263-7265
www.medcoassociates.com

Med-Expertise, L.L.C.
7000 Regency Square, Suite 225
Houston, TX 77036
713-914-0112
Fax: 713-914-0162
www.med-expertise.com

Medical Legal Consultants
11727 Kiowa Avenue, Suite 1
Los Angeles, CA 90049
808-661-3595
Fax: 808-667-6229
www.mlegal.com

Medical Liability Consultants
2015 Enterprise Avenue
League City, TX 77573
281-334-5166
Fax: 281-334-7712
www.malpractice.us.com

Medical Review Foundation, Inc.
120 Beulah Road, N.E., Suite 200
Vienna, VA 22180
800-336-0332
Fax: 703-255-6134
www.malpracticeexperts.com

Medical Review Institute of America
PO Box 2670
Salt Lake City, UT 84110-2670
801-261-3003
800-654-2422
Fax: 801-261-3189

Medilex, Inc.
175 East 96th Street, Suite 8H
New York, NY 10128-6204
212-860-8700
Fax: 212-860-8263
www.medilex.net

medQuest, Ltd.
116 East 30th Street
New York, NY 10016
212-725-8000
800-633-6251
Fax: 212-725-5090
www.medquestltd.com

National Forensic Center
17 Temple Terrace
Lawrenceville, NJ 08648
609-883-0550
800-526-5177
Fax: 609-883-7622
www.expertindex.com

Physicians for Quality
PO Box 730
Boerne, TX 78006
800-284-3627
Fax: 830-537-4052
www.pfq.com

Pro/Consul
1714 East Bethany Home Road
Phoenix, AZ 85016
800-392-1119
Fax: 602-604-9454
www.pro-consul.com

PsyBar L.L.C.
4500 Park Glen Road, Suite 330
St. Louis Park, MN 55416
952-285-9000
Fax: 952-848-1798
www.psybar.com

Summit Professional Resources LLC
486 Schooley's Mountain Road
Building 2A, Suite 11
Hackettstown, NJ 07840-4000
908-852-9008
Fax: 908-852-8003
www.summitresources.com

TAB Consultant Registry
Technical Assistance Bureau, Inc.
11469 Olive Boulevard, Suite 108
800-260-8174
Fax: 314-273-5779
www.tabexperts.com

TASA Directory of Expertise
Technical Advisory Service
for Attorneys
1166 DeKalb Pike
Blue Bell, PA 19422-1853
800-523-2319
Fax: 800-329-8272
www.tasanet.com

**Technical Network
Consulting Service**
620 Sentry Parkway, Suite 130
Blue Bell, PA 19422
610-941-3981
800-355-1329
Fax: 610-941-9730
www.techmedexperts.com

**Internet Expert Witness
Directories/Referral Services**

www.diligenceinc.com
Diligence Incorporated

www.expertmedicalwitnesses.com
Expert Medical Witnesses, Inc.

www.expertnetwork.com
The Legal Expert Network

www.experts-on-line.com
Experts-on-Line

www.lexpertresearch.com
Lexpert Research Services

www.medicallyspeaking.com
Medically Speaking

www.mlegal.com
MedicoLegal Consultants

www.unirisk.com
Unirisk Expert Witness Services

www.witness.net
Expert Witness Network

**Professional Association
Referral Services**

Your specialty association or
society may refer attorneys to its
members. Make the administrator
aware that you do litigation
support work. Also, many professional associations now post their
membership information online
for referral purposes.

ECI BOOKSTORE

You can order these expert witness training materials using the order form at the back of the book, or at www.expertcommunications.com. All products carry a money-back satisfaction guarantee.

Books

The Comprehensive Forensic Services Manual: The Essential Resources for All Experts – © 2000
    Steven Babitsky, JD;
    James J. Mangraviti, Jr., JD; &
    Christopher J. Todd, JD
                    — $124.99

The definitive "how-to" work on expert witnessing. *The Comprehensive Forensic Services Manual* contains over 400 examples with answers to the most vexing problems experts face, including:

- How to best connect with and persuade a jury
- How to market yourself professionally and cost-effectively
- Premium fee-setting, billing, and collection techniques
- Expert witness risk management
- How to handle abuse by attorneys
- How to maintain high ethical standards
- Bullet-proofing your *c.v.* and written reports
- Meeting challenges under Daubert
- The limits of discovery and privilege

The Expert Witness Handbook: Tips and Techniques for the Litigation Consultant – © 1997
    Dan Poynter
                    — $39.95

The Expert Witness Handbook is for every professional who wants an exciting new career as well as every expert witness who wants to serve more professionally and more successfully. This book describes the necessary qualifications, shows you how to break into the business and then takes you step by step in dealing with attorneys, judges, and juries. Written by a practicing expert of more than 25 years, this book is full of the inside nuts-and-bolts tips only a participant could know.

Succeeding as an Expert Witness: Increasing Your Impact and Income – © 2000
    Harold A. Feder, ESQ.
                    — $39.95

Are you prepared to use what you already know to generate extra income? You'll find all the information you need in this highly acclaimed text to embark on what could very well become a lucrative second career as a successful expert. Learn what to do, how to prepare, what to expect, and how to get started. The author was a noted trial lawyer who achieved favorable results by retaining experts throughout his trial career. This third printing of *Succeeding as an Expert* now has 30% more information.

How to Excel During Depositions: Techniques for Experts that Work – © 1999
    Steven Babitsky, ESQ. &
    James J. Mangraviti, Jr., ESQ.
                    — $59.95

An indispensable resource for all experts, *How to Excel During Depositions* has been written as a companion volume to the authors' best-selling text *How to Excel During Cross-Examination. How to Excel During Depositions* clearly and simply explains exactly what to do and what not to do during all phases of the deposition process including: scheduling, preparation, dealing with documents and subpoenas, answering counsel's questions, avoiding abuse, and collecting your fee.

The authors teach by example and have included over 150 examples of question and answer exchanges from depositions. Each example contains a *lesson* in which the authors emphasize what should be learned from it. Also included are a detailed index, deposition checklist, select Federal Rules of Civil Procedure, and much more.

How to Excel During Cross-Examination: Techniques for Experts that Work – © 1997
    Steven Babitsky, ESQ. &
    James J. Mangraviti, Jr., ESQ.
                    — $59.95

This new practical survival guide for expert witnesses reveals all of the techniques and *tricks* used by trial attorneys during cross-examination. Each technique is identified,

explained, and illustrated with actual and sample trial testimony. As an expert witness, your *marketability* will increase dramatically once you master cross-examination. Attorneys seek out expert witnesses who excel during cross-examination.

Writing and Defending Your Expert Report: The Step-by-Step Guide with Models – © 2002
    Steven Babitsky, ESQ. &
    James J. Mangraviti, Jr., ESQ.
                    — $99.95

Your expert opinion is only as strong as your expert report. Opposing counsel can and will use every tactic, fair and unfair, to turn your own report against you. A well-written report is your first and best line of defense from such attacks. Equally important is your ability to recognize counsel's tactics and neutralize them. *Writing and Defending Your Expert Report: The Step-by-Step Guide with Models* is the seminal work on how to craft and confidently and expertly defend your expert report.

The Guide to Experts' Fees: Results of a Survey by The National Forensic Center – © 2002
    Betty S. Lipscher, Director
                    — $29.95

The National Forensic Center surveyed experts in many fields to ascertain their current charges and fees. Questionnaires were sent to randomly selected specialists listed in the Forensic Services Directory. The result is this valuable indication of experts' fees across the country.

The Guide to Experts' Fees is intended as a general reference to assist experts and attorneys. Because fees vary so widely, even among experts in the same specialty, the *Guide* includes high, low, and average fees for trial preparation and testimony, reports, depositions, graphics, and dispute resolution within each area of expertise.

The Independent Medical Evaluation Report: A Step-by-Step Guide with Models – © 1996
Christopher R. Brigham, MD; Steven Babitsky, JD; & James J. Mangraviti, Jr., JD
— $99.95

This best-seller text provides the physician with the information needed to prepare and write top quality independent medical evaluation reports. The authors teach by example and have included complete copies of ten model independent medical evaluation reports.

The Comprehensive IME System: Essential Resources for an Efficient and Successful IME Practice – © 1997
Christopher R. Brigham, MD
— $459.00

This unique, comprehensive system permits you to make the most effective use of your time, enhance dramatically the value and quality of your evaluations, and increase the demand for your premium valued services. Based on our years of experience in this field, we have developed the resources and tools essential for a successful independent medical examination (IME) practice. The system is comprised of a 300-page resource text and accompanying diskettes.

This is an integrated system comprised of over 40 key resources, including: IME process checklist, referral form, notification letter, examinee questionnaire, pain drawing and various pain and disability inventories, report template, preliminary report, release form, fee calculation worksheet, standardized letters, marketing resources, and much more. These resources are also provided on diskettes (IBM PC, in WordPerfect 6.0/6.1 and Microsoft Word 8.0/Word 97 formats). The use of these resources is explained in the text, which details the necessary steps to performing a quality evaluation and achieving a successful IME practice.

Audiotapes

Law School for Experts: Audio Program – © 2000
James J. Mangraviti, Jr., ESQ.
— $124.99

The highly acclaimed *Law School for Experts* seminar is now available on audiotape. This course provides you with the fundamental legal knowledge you need in order to excel as an expert. *Law School for Experts* is presented in a lively fashion and features dozens of examples, questions and answers. It was recorded live at an expert witness seminar and was rated 4.9 out of a possible 5.0 by the attendees at that seminar.

Law School for Experts includes five and one-half hours of lively audio on six cassettes plus a 154-page, text-quality seminar manual, which follows the audio presentations.

Marketing Your Forensic Practice: How to Increase Your Business in a Cost-Effective, Professional Manner – © 1999
>   Steven Babitsky, ESQ.;
>   Rosalie Hamilton;
>   James J. Mangraviti, Jr., ESQ.; &
>   Matt Carpenter
>   — $124.99

Discover how to promote your services in a cost-effective and dignified manner. *Marketing Your Forensic Practice* is presented by an expert faculty with over 50 years' combined experience in this area. They explain exactly what works, what will not work, and the marketing techniques and strategies that may be best for your particular practice. Includes six audiocassettes with over five hours of lively audio and a detailed, 89-page written manual. You will learn dozens of cost-effective marketing techniques that can be used to dramatically increase your business, how to charge and collect a premium for your time, how to design professional marketing material that will not generate a backlash, the three golden rules of forensic marketing, how to promote yourself via the Internet, how attorneys locate and select experts, and much, much more.

Achieve Success as an Effective Medical Witness – SEAK, INC.
>   — $189.95

This outstanding audiotape program provides you with the fastest, most cost-effective and easiest way for you to master the skills needed for testifying as a medical witness and being an expert consultant. It has been designed by SEAK, Inc. and the nation's leading legal and medical-legal experts to help you achieve success as a medical witness. The comprehensive package includes six audiocassette tapes and resource manual that provides information covered in the tape series, as well as learning exercises and a code of ethics.

How to be a Successful Independent Medical Examiner: The Distance Learning Program – © 2000
>   Christopher R. Brigham, MD
>   — $249.95

This highly acclaimed program will teach you how to be more effective, efficient, and successful as an independent medical examiner. A wealth of information is presented in a very lively fashion by Christopher R. Brigham, MD, CIME, the founder of the American Board of Independent Medical Examiners and the Editor-in-Chief of the *AMA Guides Newsletter*. This program provides practical solutions to everyday problems and challenges associated with IMEs, such as dealing with challenging examinees, minimizing risks and liabilities, assessing symptom magnification and malingering, structuring your practice in the most cost-effective manner, writing excellent reports, better promoting your expertise, and generating and collecting a premium fee in a timely manner. Specific action steps are provided which you can immediately implement to make your IME practice more successful. The program includes a 190-page resource manual, which follows the presentations and includes sample reports, report templates, pain inventories, practice management forms, and much more.

Achieving Success with Workers' Compensation – SEAK, INC.
— $189.95

Designed by SEAK and the nation's top experts to help you gain the needed knowledge and skills for success in the Workers' Compensation arena at minimum expense and effort. Extensive package includes six hour-long audiotapes, resource manual, and PC compatible forms diskette.

Videotapes

Winning Over the Jury: Techniques for Experts that Work – © 2001
Steven Babitsky, ESQ. & James J. Mangraviti, Jr., ESQ.
— $95.00

The true value of any expert testimony depends solely on what weight the expert's testimony is given by the jury. This program contains dozens of proven and advanced techniques, which show experts how to connect with and win over the jury. The program teaches by example and contains over 75 examples, which clearly demonstrate what to do and what not to do in front of a jury.

The Most Difficult Questions for Experts: With Answers – © 2000
Steven Babitsky, ESQ. & James J. Mangraviti, Jr., ESQ.
— $95.00

This 47-minute videotape reveals the 50 most challenging trick and difficult questions an expert will face during cross-examination. Attorney Jim Mangraviti explains the tactical reasons a cross-examiner may ask each question. Courtroom demonstrations present truthful, artful answers which will prevent the cross-examiner from unfairly twisting your testimony and misleading the jury. This tape teaches you how to rebuff the cross-examining attorney's trick questions.

The Expert Deposition: How to be an Effective and Ethical Witness (For All Non-Medical Experts) – © 1999
Steven Babitsky, ESQ. & James J. Mangraviti, Jr., ESQ.
— $95.00

This video is an indispensable resource for all experts in non-medical fields, by the authors of *How to Excel During Depositions* and *How To Excel During Cross-Examination. The Expert Deposition* clearly and simply explains what to do and what not to do during all phases of the deposition process – scheduling, preparation, dealing with documents and subpoenas, answering counsel's questions, avoiding abuse, and collecting your fee. Each video demonstrates by example and includes over 40 examples of question and answer exchanges. The video depicts common exchanges between lawyers and health professionals. Each example illustrates one or more points made during the tape.

Cross-Examination: How to be an Effective and Ethical Expert Witness – © 2000
Steven Babitsky, ESQ. & James J. Mangraviti, Jr., ESQ.
— $95.00

This 59-minute videotape teaches you how to give mistake-free cross-examination testimony. The tape demonstrates by example and features over 50 lively cross-examination exchanges between lawyer and expert witness. Each example features one or more points made during the tape.

Preparing for Your Deposition: Advanced Training for Anyone Testifying at Deposition or Trial – © 1998
Moderated by
David M. Benjamin, PH.D.
Clinical Pharmacologist and Toxicologist; Fellow, American College of Legal Medicine
— $149.00

This two-hour video has been condensed from the proceedings of the 1998 Medical and Forensic Experts Conference. The theme of the conference was "Dealing with Abusive Depositions and Aggressive Cross-Examination." The enclosures are from the conference syllabus, and the video includes questions,

comments, and analyses from physicians, experts, and attorney faculty members, as well as attorneys and experts who attended. The video includes instruction on recognizing and dealing with trick questions and abusive tactics at deposition, and examples of actual deposition testimony, specifically selected to clear up common misunderstandings and illustrate both good and bad responses to questions.

Surviving Cross Examination: Advanced Training for Anyone Testifying at Deposition or Trial – © 1998
Moderated by
David M. Benjamin, PH.D.
Clinical Pharmacologist and Toxicologist; Fellow, American College of Legal Medicine
— $149.00

This two-hour video has been condensed from the proceedings of the 1998 Medical and Forensic Experts Conference. The theme of the conference was "Dealing with Abusive Depositions and Aggressive Cross-Examination." The enclosures are from the conference syllabus, and the video includes questions, comments, and analyses from physicians, experts, and attorney faculty members, as well as attorneys and experts who attended. The video includes a mock "Daubert Hearing" in which two experts are cross-examined about the reliability of their opinions. Only one expert's opinions were admitted, and you get to be the Judge!

INDEX

Insurance, expert witness 12, 59–60
Internet 29, 177–192
Introductory letter 89–92, 133–134, 142
Invisible Touch, The 102
Invoice — See Billing

Judicial fundraisers 105

Law schools 106
Lawyers Weekly USA Study 97
Legal issues, business 12–13, 59–60
Logo — See Brand

Mailing list — See Database
Mailing list cleaning 70
Mailing list of attorneys 64, 66, 135
Mailing service 141
Marketing plan 16–22
Marketing, definition of 3
Media consultants 119, 129–130
Media kit 78, 129

Nametags 111–112
National advertising 164–165, 174, 177
Networking 97–112, 199
News release 120–129
Newsletter 133, 137–139

Photograph 76, 83, 88, 183
Planning — See Business plan and
   Marketing plan
Positioning statement —
   See Statement of profession
Postal information 140–141
Postcard — See Professional
   announcement
Press kit — See Media kit
Press release — See News release
Professional announcement 64, 66,
   120–125, 133, 136–137, 160, 187

Prospect targeting 15–16, 64, 134, 156
Public relations 22, 129
Publicity 115–130

Radio — See Electronic media
Referral service 45, 145–150, 201–202
Referrals 64–66, 75, 97–100, 142, 200
Response letter —
   See Inquiry response letter
Resume — See Curriculum Vitae
Retainer 38–39, 50, 92
Rolodex® card 78

Search engine 179, 184–186, 190
Selling the Invisible 4, 103
Services 14, 19
Solicitation letter — See Introductory letter
Speaking 117–118, 130, 199
Statement of profession 107–108
Stationery 78–79, 181, 187

TASA (Technical Advisory Service for
   Attorneys) 21, 147
Telephone communication 65–66, 68, 94
Thank-you notes 100–101, 104
Time sheet 42, 44
Trade shows — See Exhibiting
TV — See Electronic media

URL — See Domain name
USP (Unique selling proposition) 108

Web site 177–192
Web site design 181–186, 188, 191–192
Web site host 180–181
Web site links 184
Web site name — See Domain name
Writing 115–117, 130

Illustrations

ABOUT THE AUTHOR

Rosalie Hamilton has worked in sales, marketing, advertising and publishing for more than twenty years. She was the Expert Witness Marketing Coordinator for *Texas Lawyer* newspaper and then its parent company, American Lawyer Media (now the National Law Journal), where she wrote *EXPERTS* newsletter, sold advertising to experts, and published expert witness directories. Through her consulting business, Expert Communications, she advises experts throughout the United States on marketing. She enjoys helping experts develop their litigation practice and speaks on legal marketing issues at expert witness conferences. A native and lifelong resident of Texas, she now lives in Clearwater, Florida.

ORDER FORM — Books Audiotapes Videotapes

Please send the following items:

Title	Price
Subtotal	
Tax (7% for Florida residents only)	
Shipping $5.00 per item	
Total	

NAME

COMPANY NAME

ADDRESS

CITY   STATE   ZIP

TELEPHONE NUMBER

Check enclosed or   ☐ Visa   ☐ MasterCard   ☐ AMEX   ☐ Discover

CARD NUMBER   EXP. DATE

NAME ON CARD

Mail, phone, fax, or email order to
  Expert Communications
  140 Island Way, #288
  Clearwater, FL 33767
  727-467-0700
  Orders: Toll-free phone 866-467-0801
          Fax 727-467-0800
          Email order@expertcommunications.com

Thank you. Your satisfaction is money-back guaranteed.